the Portable Needlepoint Boutique

the Portable Needlepoint Boutique

JOYCE AIKEN

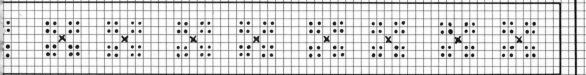

Taplinger Publishing Company ‖ New York

By Joyce Aiken and Jean Ray Laury

CREATING BODY COVERINGS

HANDMADE RUGS FROM PRACTICALLY ANYTHING

THE TOTAL TOTE BAG BOOK

•   •   •   •

First Edition

Published in the United States in 1977 by
TAPLINGER PUBLISHING CO., INC.
New York, New York

Published simultaneously in the Dominion of Canada by
Burns & MacEachern Limited, Ontario

Library of Congress Cataloging in Publication Data

Aiken, Joyce
   The portable needlepoint boutique.

   1. Canvas embroidery. I. Title.
TT778.C3A47 1977   746.4'4   76-53870

ISBN 0-8008-6416-6

Black and white photographs are by the author;
color photographs are by Jim Heitzeberg

Designed by Mollie M. Torras

Acknowledgments

My special thanks to LaMina Smith who contributed her multi-striped purse and also helped stitch many of the designs used in this book. Thanks also to Jean Ray Laury for the design of her Christmas tree angel ornament.

I especially appreciate Jim Heitzeberg's color photography, and the help and advice he has given me, as well as the patience shown by my editor, Bobs Pinkerton.

Contents

Color Plates follow page 64

Foreword

Sit down in the waiting room of a dentist's office or buckle up in an airplane seat and, on cue, out come the familiar needlepoint materials—canvas, yarn, and tiny scissors. More and more people are finding this a rewarding and relaxing way to spend those in-between moments during a busy day. The small and easy-to-carry project has become a favorite with needlepointers. A few stitches worked into a canvas while under the hair dryer or at the doctor's office can make the difference between a finished project or one waiting to be stitched at home.

Many of the projects in this book are designed to organize, store, or identify the special or everyday item. A needlepoint luggage tag easily identifies your bag and is much more attractive than the plastic snap-ons the airlines give away. A roll-up manicure case gathers all the needed tools together and a small sewing kit is ready for an emergency at any time. Christmas ornaments appear only in December but will be welcomed for years to come.

The new interlock canvas gives you the opportunity to cut openings in the mesh or right next to a yarn edge without concern about raveling threads. Some of the designs will show you new techniques that you can incorporate into larger stay-at-home projects. Beginners will find the directions and full-size patterns easy to follow; advanced stitchers can try new designs. It is fun to get away from some of the tried and true projects. You will not find an eyeglasses case or pillow-top design, but you will find a contact-lens case and a desk set. You will also discover a jewelry case, hatband, sewing kit, candleholder, camera case, and more. So, stitch away.

Joyce Aiken

Needlepoint Basics

Materials

Only the best materials available should be used for needle-point. It doesn't pay to work hours on a project if the yarns and canvas are inferior. If there is no specialty shop in your town for needlepoint supplies, a department store should be able to provide what you need.

Canvas

All projects in the book are worked on #12 mono or interlock canvas, 12 squares to the inch. A #10 or #14 canvas with 10 or 14 squares to-the-inch can be used for some projects, but those that are charted for lettering or use a graphed design are planned for #12 canvas and will change in size if another canvas is used.

Mono canvas is woven with single threads to form the mesh and is the most popular canvas available. Machine stitching is required at the edges after blocking to keep the threads from raveling.

Interlock canvas has two vertical threads that twine around each horizontal thread. It is more ridged than mono canvas and does not ravel at a cut edge. It is the only canvas available that allows you to cut next to the yarn and finish the edge with an over-cast stitch. The projects that call for overcast edges must be done with interlock canvas.

Needles

Tapestry needles have blunt points that slide through the mesh without splitting the canvas threads. A #18 needle is suitable for working on #10 or #12 canvas. If you work on #14 canvas, choose a #20 tapestry needle. The needles have large eyes for ease in threading. Just fold the yarn over the needle and pull tight. Pinch the folded yarn between your fingers, slip the needle out, and thread the folded yarn end through the eye.

Yarn

The most suitable yarn for needlepoint is persian wool. The wool is loosely twisted into three strands of yarn that can easily be separated for use on different size canvas. A #12 or #14 canvas requires two strands of yarn. You can either thread two pieces of yarn on the needle and leave the ends loose, or use one piece of yarn doubled over with no loose ends. A #10 canvas requires three strands of yarn to adequately cover the canvas. The estimate of yarn required for all projects in this book is based on Paternayan persian yarn. It is available in many colors and is sold in most needlepoint shops by the ounce or small skein (about 9 yards). The yarn in each skein is usually cut in 33-inch or 66-inch lengths. All yarn calculations have been figured for 33-inch-long strands. If you purchase yarn in 66-inch lengths, cut yarn requirements in half—instead of twenty 33-inch-long pieces of one color, buy ten 66-inch-long pieces.

Preparation

Careful preparation of needlepoint materials is as important as careful stitching. Read the information in this section thoroughly before proceeding with your project.

Preparing Canvas

The dimensions of the canvas are given in all the instructions. After cutting the canvas, bind the edges with 1-inch masking tape to keep yarn from catching on the thread ends. The canvas should be even in weave and free of knots or tied threads. Place your pattern with the selvage on the side—not the top or bottom. The canvas mesh may look even, but there is usually a difference in thread space between horizontal and vertical threads. If more than one piece of canvas is used in a project, be sure the direction is the same for both.

Transferring Design

All designs in the book are full-size on 12-to-the-inch grids. Trace the design from the book, place your canvas over the drawing, and use one of the techniques mentioned below to transfer to

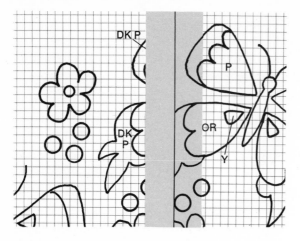

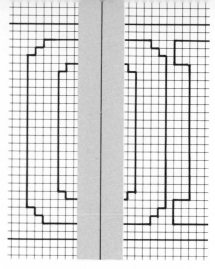

Division of a black-graphed design

Gray-graphed design divided across pages with small design area repeated in solid gray at right

canvas. The pattern should be centered on the canvas so that there is at least a 1½-inch border on all edges.

It is not necessary to painstakingly chart each design on graph paper and then transfer it to canvas. Most designs can be transferred to canvas from a simple drawing.

When patterns are too large for a single page they are placed on two facing pages. Those on black graphs are divided in the middle of a square with a gray band between. For those designs drawn on gray graphs a portion of the design is repeated on the right-hand page over the solid gray band between. Then they can be traced; the tracing is overlapped to form a continuous design.

Until marking pens made especially for needlepoint became available, many stitchers used any permanent marking pen they could find to outline a design—some still do. These pens are not always as permanent as their manufacturers claim. The ink sometimes bleeds into the yarn when the canvas is blocked. To test the permanence of such a pen, draw on a scrap of canvas, let the ink dry completely, iron the canvas (heat helps set the color), and, finally, put it in water and try to rub off the ink. If there is no smearing, it is okay. It sounds like a lot of work, but it's not as much as if you had to restitch a design because the yarn became discolored during blocking. Never use a ball-point pen or graphite pencil—they both rub off. Probably the safest medium for outlining a design is gray acrylic paint, thinned enough to brush easily onto canvas.

Graphed Designs

Some geometric patterns require use of a graphed design. It is not necessary to transfer the design to canvas. Simply count the blocked-out squares of the graph in each color. When working this way, the only marking needed on the canvas is the outline shape of the design.

Lettering is always charted on a graph. Here are three different styles and sizes of alphabets. When planning placement of a line of words on canvas, count the spaces needed for each letter, add a space or two between each one (more between words), and divide

Two needlepoint alphabets—small letters and capitals

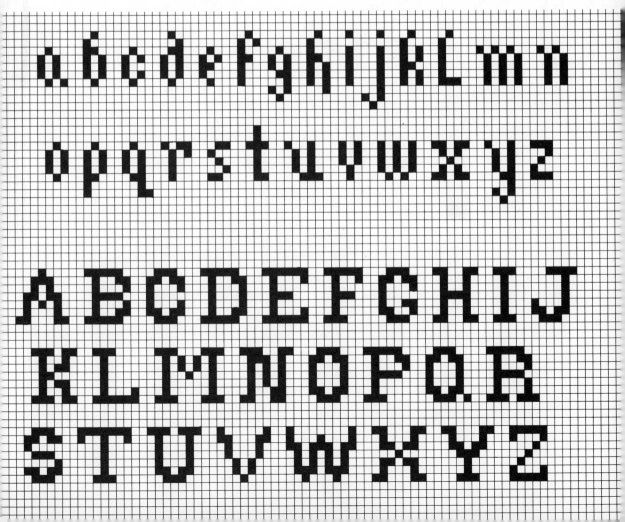

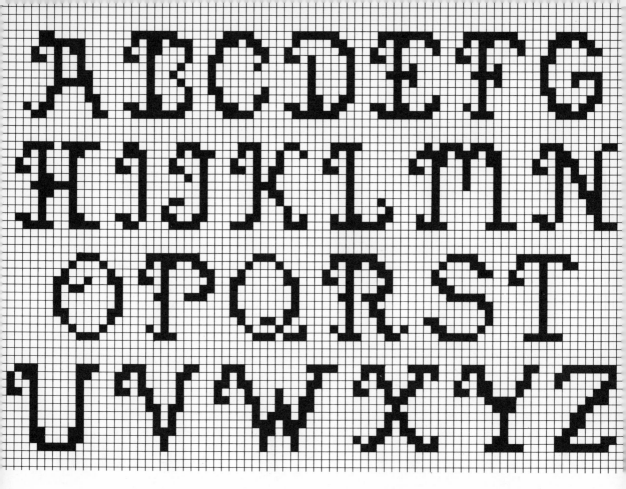

A more intricate needlepoint alphabet

the total in half. Locate the center of canvas and allot half of the counted spaces to each side of the center. It may be necessary to work lettering backwards from the center to the left-hand edge.

Clustered Patterns

Small patterns like coasters can be drawn on one piece of canvas, using less canvas than if each design is put on a separate piece. Allow 1½ inches for the border edge and 1½ inches between each design. Block the canvas as a whole, and cut it apart after needlepoint is dry and ready for finishing.

Staining Canvas

Coloring the canvas is not absolutely required before stitching, but it is best to do so. Coloring the canvas makes it easier to see changes in yarn color and keeps the white threads of the canvas from showing through the stitching. If you stain the canvas with paint, be sure the color is thinned enough or it will clog the holes in the canvas. When an edge is to be turned, stain the canvas a few rows outside the outline. This helps to hide any threads that might be exposed in turning.

Acrylic paint is one of the best colorings to use on canvas. It is thinned with water, and, once it is dry, the color is permanent. A basic beginner's set of paints will provide enough colors for mixing most yarn shades. With the marking pens made especially for needlepoint there is no way to mix colors.

Oil paint is a traditional stain for canvas; turpentine is used to thin the color. The drying time of oil is longer than that of acrylics, however, so there will be a waiting period before starting the work.

Regular crayons, not the washable kind, also work well as a stain. After applying a light coat of color to the canvas, put a piece of tissue paper over the design and heat it with an iron. The crayon will melt into the canvas threads and will not bleed when wet.

Stitching Design

All projects shown in the book are worked with one of the basic tent stitches—basketweave or continental. Both look the same on the front of the canvas, but are stitched by different methods. Occasionally, a cross-stitch is used in a design to emphasize a single dot of color, and the overcast stitch is used to finish the cut edge of some projects.

Basketweave Stitch

The basketweave stitch is the most desirable of the tent stitches. It does not require turning the canvas upside down as you work, and it does not distort the canvas as much as the continental stitch.

Start the stitch in the upper right-hand corner of the design. Bring the needle up from the back of the canvas through point #1. Put the needle through the front of the canvas to the back at point #2. Let the needle travel to #3 and come back to the front of the canvas. Follow the drawing, bringing the needle up from the back on odd numbers and down through the front on even numbers. Rows of basketweave are always on the diagonal. As you stitch up a row from right to left, your needle moves across the back of the canvas in a horizontal position as shown in the drawing. When you work down a row from left to right, your needle will move in a vertical position, as shown in the second drawing. Beginners have the greatest difficulty starting a new row of stitching. Remember that the first stitch of a new row, starting at the top, begins one square immediately to the left of the last stitch taken. The first stitch at the beginning of a new row at the bottom begins immediately below the last stitch taken.

Never finish a thread at the end of a row; it will be difficult to know at which end of the row to start a new thread. If two rows are stitched together in the same direction, an uneven ridge may appear in the needlepoint surface.

Needle positions in basketweave stitch

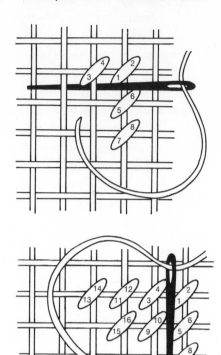

Continental Stitch

This is an easier stitch to learn than the basketweave, but has certain disadvantages. The canvas must be turned upside down at the end of each row even if the row is only three stitches long. It also distorts canvas more than basketweave, so it may be necessary to block the work more than once. The continental stitch is useful for filling in irregular areas where the basketweave would be difficult to stitch.

Start the stitch in the upper right-hand corner of the design. Bring the needle up from the back of the canvas through point #1. Put the needle

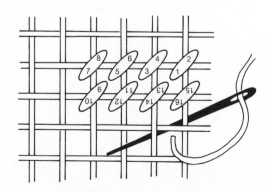

Continental stitching

through the canvas at point #2 and travel across the back of the canvas to point #3. Bring the needle through point #3 and to the front of the canvas. Follow the drawing, going from the front to back on even numbers and from the back to front on odd numbers. Stitching always goes from right to left. At the end of each row turn the canvas upside down before beginning a new row. This maintains the right-to-left direction in stitching.

Cross-stitch

Cross-stitching

The cross-stitch is used in a number of projects where a single stitch is to be emphasized and given a padded look. Doubling up of yarn in one stitch gives it greater height and fuller color.

The first half of the stitch is a regular continental stitch, the second half crosses over the first stitch to form an X. It is desirable to work all the first stitches in one direction so that all the second stitches slant the same way.

Overcast Stitch

This is the stitch used to finish the cut edge of interlock canvas. It binds the edge and makes it possible to finish a design without having to turn the canvas edge under. The hatband and luggage tags are among the designs that use this stitch.

Work the design to one row from the pattern edge. Block the needlepoint and trim the excess canvas to one row outside the last

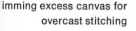
imming excess canvas for
overcast stitching

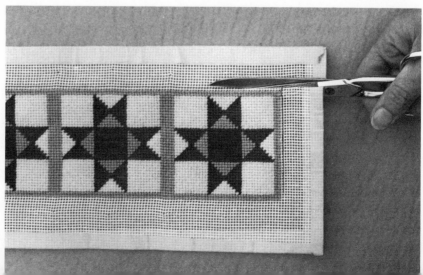

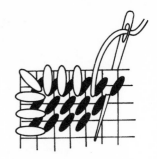

Overcast stitching
on corners

Overcast stitching the canvas

row of stitching. Overcast stitch through the last row of stitching and over the cut edge. To cover canvas adequately at the corners, stitch three times in the same hole. If a double strand of yarn does not cover the edge, add one more strand of yarn to your needle.

Stitching Hints

When starting to stitch on a new canvas or in an isolated color area, insert your needle into the front of the canvas, about 1 inch away from the first stitch, but in the path of the color you are working with. Leave a tail of yarn, about ½ of an inch long, on the front of canvas. After working a few rows, the yarn will have been caught on the back of the canvas, and you can pull the yarn end to the back and cut it off. This method keeps yarn ends from tangling in the stitching.

When all but 3 inches of yarn have been used, take thread to the back of canvas and run the needle under a stitched area for ½ of an inch. Clip off threads close to the canvas. The back of the canvas should be free of yarn ends so that they will not be pulled to the front of canvas while stitching.

If you begin a new thread next to an area already stitched, start by running the needle under a few of the existing stitches on the back of the canvas next to the new working area.

As you stitch, the yarn may tighten its twist, making it smaller in diameter and covering less of the canvas threads. Occasionally drop the needle and yarn and let them spin so that the yarn fluffs out again.

Everyone stitches with a different tension. This may change the amount of yarn used in each design. If you find you are running out of yarn before completing the design, adjust the amount of yarn needed for each pattern.

The canvas may "shrink" as the stitches pull the canvas tight. Add a row or two of stitching around the outside edge if the measurement is critical.

Be sure that all the yarn of one color in your project is from the same dye lot. Check yarn when it is purchased, since the shop may have two dye lots of the same color on hand.

Stitch lettering and small color areas first; the background should be stitched last. It is much easier to see the design when it is free of background yarn.

Work with clean hands and wash them occasionally while stitching. Oil from your hands will change the color of light yarns. White and yellow are especially susceptible to color changes from handling. For example, just moving a newspaper aside will leave enough ink on your hands to affect the yarn.

Blocking

All projects will require blocking because diagonal tent stitches tend to pull the canvas out of shape. Blocking is not difficult and the materials needed to do it are usually available at home. The back of a breadboard is fine for blocking small projects. If you don't have a breadboard, find a pine board that is soft enough to push pins into. Cover the board with a clean dish towel or cotton fabric. Place needlepoint facedown on the cloth and pin one edge to the board. Dampen the back of canvas with a sponge, until the yarn is saturated with water. Now pull the canvas into shape, pinning the edges as it straightens. Be sure to use aluminum pushpins or stainless steel T pins that do not rust. Pins are put into the canvas edge and not into the yarn stitching.

If design outline is irregular in shape, make a paper pattern matching the stitched area and use it to guide you in blocking. Lay the pattern on top of the stretched and pinned needlepoint to check the outline; adjust if necessary.

Keep the needlepoint flat while it is drying so that moisture remains evenly distributed in the yarn. Allow it to dry completely before removing it from the board. Do not shorten the drying time by placing needlepoint in front of a heater. It may take overnight for the canvas to completely dry and, if the canvas is badly distorted, blocking may have to be repeated.

Blocking needlepoint design on the back of a breadboard

Finishing

The difference between an amateur and a professional look to needlepoint lies in the way it was finished. Specific directions for finishing are given with each project. Some patterns require joining with machine stitching; many can be completed by hand sewing. It is well worth spending a few extra minutes to carefully finish a project you've spent hours working on.

Edges

After blocking, remove needlepoint from the board and trim the excess canvas from edges. Each project will specify how much of an edge to leave, from ½ of an inch to 1 inch. Mono canvas requires a row of machine stitching at the edge to keep the threads from raveling. Use a zigzag or double row of straight stitching on the canvas, just outside the yarn edge.

Whipstitching

This stitch is used to join two edges of needlepoint with a single row of stitching. It resembles a satin stitch in embroidery.

After needlepoint is blocked and the excess canvas is trimmed, turn the canvas edges to the back, leaving one line of canvas thread exposed on each side to be joined. Baste in place. Start at one end of one side and catch a thread of canvas on both edges. Work back and forth, stitching in each hole on each side, until the entire seam is joined, as shown in the drawing. Keep rows of canvas even so that the last stitch on each side lines up.

The whipstitch is also used to join the edges of a needlepoint project that is to be slipped over another form; this is done with the candleholder base and the pencil holder, for example. When working over an object, start the whipstitch at the top edge and work down ½ of an inch before slipping the needlepoint onto the form. Secure the canvas around the form with rubber bands, and continue stitching to the bottom.

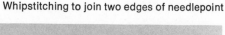

Whipstitching to join two edges of needlepoint

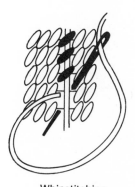

Whipstitching

Machine-stitched Seams

Finished needlepoint can be treated the same way as any heavy upholstery fabric with regard to machine sewing. With right sides facing, baste together, trying to match yarn rows if possible. With a long stitch, machine-sew two rows inside the yarn edge.

Lacing

Lacing is used to hold needlepoint canvas in place over a rigid form when gluing is not desired. After blocking and machine-stitching the edges, trim the canvas as instructed. A heavy carpet thread should be used to lace canvas to the form. Sew through the canvas, between the machine stitching and the yarn edge. Travel back and forth across the back, first in one direction and then in the other.

Lacing back and forth

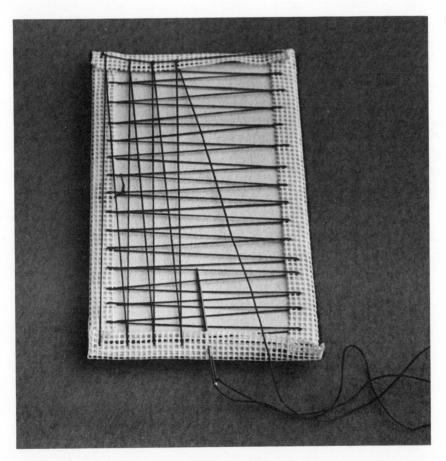

Gluing

Glue is a great help in finishing some projects. A flexible glue made for fabric or needlepoint should be used, since all-purpose glues tend to become hard when they dry and will affect the yarn if applied too heavily. Spread fabric glue on lightly so that it will not work through the canvas and into the yarn. When necessary, pushpins or rubber bands can hold canvas in place while the glue dries.

Linings

Lining fabrics should be chosen for their use. Felt is a non-woven fabric that does not ravel when cut. It is ideal for backing irregular shapes or flat projects that are not handled much. Purse linings should be smoothly textured. Carrying cases, such as the manicure case, need a lining that keeps tools from slipping out of place. A twill or textured cotton is suitable for this. Grosgrain ribbon is ideal for lining narrow bands, such as the hatband and camera-case strap. Edges of the ribbon are finished and don't require turning.

Zippers

Small projects often call for short zippers that are difficult to find. The easiest way to solve this problem is to buy a nylon or polyester zipper and cut it ½ of an inch longer than the correct length. Whipstitch across the zipper with yarn or sewing thread at the point at which the zipper is to stop.

Loop Closures

A yarn loop (used for a closing device along with a button) can be made stronger by working a buttonhole stitch over the yarn. Measure the length needed to slip over the button. Attach a double strand of yarn of the correct length to the needlepoint for the loop. With another length of yarn, buttonhole stitch over the loop as shown. Continue stitching around the loop, covering the yarn completely.

Buttonhole stitching
to strengthen the
yarn loop

Making tassels

Tassels

Tassels can be made with needle-point yarn, rayon thread, or nicely tex-tured wools. Cut a piece of cardboard 1 inch longer than the desired length of the tassel. Wrap the yarn around the cardboard until tassel is of the proper thickness. Tie a piece of yarn around the center of wrapped yarn. Slip off cardboard, hold the hank by tied yarn, and cut the opposite end of yarn pieces. With yarn held together at the tied end, wrap and tie another piece of yarn below the top to keep tassel in place. Use the top yarn tie to attach the tassel to the needlepoint corners by slipping it between the canvas and the backing or by tying it to a canvas thread.

Metal Purse Handles

Gold and silver-colored metal handles are available in many sizes and styles for needlepoint purses. The frames have a row of holes at the edge of the rim for sewing to a needlepoint canvas. Some are made so that the needlepoint can be sewn to the top of the metal. Others have an inner metal rim so that the needlepoint can be inserted between the inner and outer edges. When buying a handle like this, be sure that the insert space is wide enough to slip a canvas edge into. Also, it is easier to sew the needlepoint to the outside of the handle.

Candleholder
Base

A wooden cube forms the base of this candleholder. Have a cube cut for you at a lumberyard, or look for the right size in the scrap barrel. This cube measures 3¼ inches on all sides. The design is a traditional quilt-block pattern and adapts well to the square shape. Other quilt designs can be used on similar-sized blocks to make up a collection of candleholders. The star on this candleholder base is light brown and blue with a dark brown center. The borders are blue and the background is white. Turn to plate 1 for color details. The finished size is 3¼ inches by 3¼ inches by 3¼ inches.

Materials
#12 interlock canvas; 1 piece, 6¼ inches by 6¼ inches,
    1 piece, 6¼ inches by 17 inches
Wooden cube
Candleholder with screw attachment and dish for dripping wax

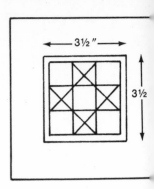

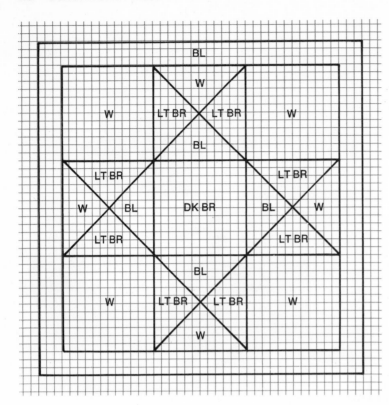

The candleholder design. The top is at the left, the side panel below. When joining the side panel sections which are separated by the gray band, allow five rows of canvas between the two units to match that between the design units on each page.

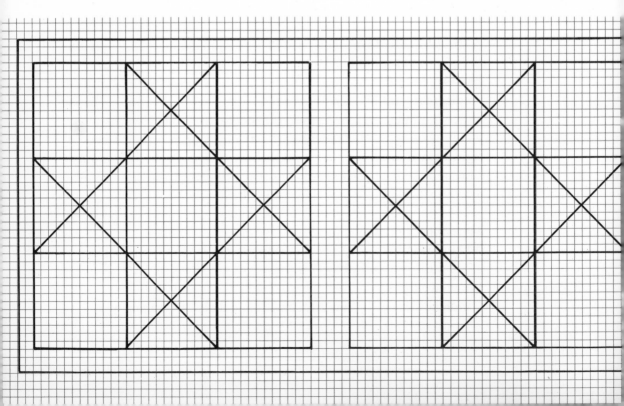

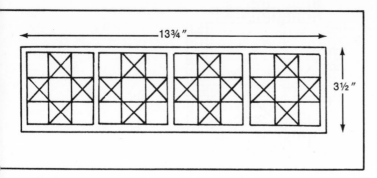

13¾″

3½″

Centering the design on pieces of canvas

Yarn   33-inch lengths
   5   dark brown   DK BR
  12   light brown   LT BR
  20   blue   BL
  25   white   W

Directions

1. Transfer the designs to the canvas, centering them so there is a generous margin. Stain or paint the designs on the canvas.
2. Stitch the star on the top square, then the blue border, and then the white background. Stitch the side panel in the same order, leaving one row unstitched on the top and bottom edges. Block both pieces of needlepoint.
3. Trim canvas to 1 inch from yarn edge on the top square. Cut corners out, as shown in the drawing on the next page.
4. Carefully cut canvas one row away from yarn stitching on top

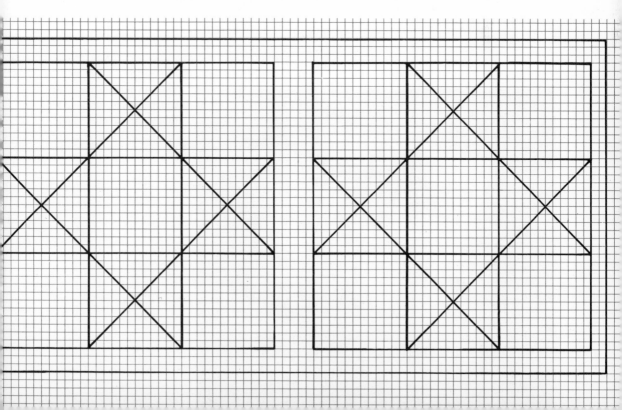

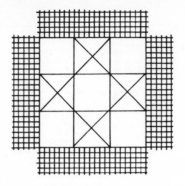

Trimming canvas and
cutting out the corners of
top piece before gluing

and bottom edges of the side panel. Cut canvas ¾ of an inch from yarn edge on each end of the side panel.

5. Overcast stitch the long edges of the side panel. Turn the canvas under on panel ends, leaving one row of canvas exposed for joining. Baste.

6. To attach the top needlepoint square, spread a light layer of glue on the top of the cube. Lay needlepoint in place so that the edges of the stitching meet the edges of the cube. Turn cube and canvas upside down, and weight the cube down with a heavy book while the glue dries.

7. When glue is dry, turn the cube upright, fold canvas edges down over cube, and glue to sides. Keep canvas in place with rubber bands, masking tape, or pushpins while glue dries.

8. Whipstitch the ends of the side panel together, ½ of an inch down from the top edge. Slip the piece onto the cube and continue stitching to the bottom.

9. Attach candleholder to the center of the top.

You can hold the top down
with pushpins, masking tape, or
rubber bands, after gluing.

Luggage Tags

Look-alike baggage is a real problem in a crowded airline terminal. Needlepoint luggage tags fulfill the airline's requirement that all baggage be identified. They also make it easy to find luggage in a hurry. Using interlock canvas makes it possible for you to cut an opening in the center of the needlepoint design for an address-label window and a small slit or eyelet for the chain. The finished sizes are 2 inches by 3½ inches. The Moroccan design is shown in color in plate 17.

Materials

#12 interlock canvas, 6½ inches by 8½ inches, for each tag
Ball link chain with connector
Small piece of clear acetate or stiff plastic

Yarn   33-inch lengths

MOROCCAN DESIGN

- 1   light brown   LT BR
- 3   dark red   DK R
- 2   tan   TAN
- 10   dark brown   DK BR

CHEVRON DESIGN

- 2   purple   PU
- 2   magenta   M
- 3   green   GR
- 9   blue   BL

Directions

1. Transfer the design to the canvas, leaving at least 1½ inches between the back and front of the tag. If you are making more than one luggage tag, cluster the designs on a piece of canvas, leaving 1½ inches between each one and around the outside edges of the canvas. Stain or paint the designs on the canvas.
2. Front: Carefully cut the small eyelet in the canvas for the chain. With border color, stitch one row away from the hole and then overcast stitch around the chain opening. Work the design, leaving one row around the outside edge unstitched.
3. Back: Cut the small eyelet for the chain and overcast stitch around the chain hole as you did for the front. Fill in the canvas with border color, leaving one row unstitched around the outside edges and around the edges of the rectangle for the address window.

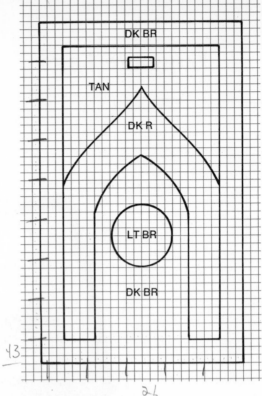

Moroccan design

Chevron design

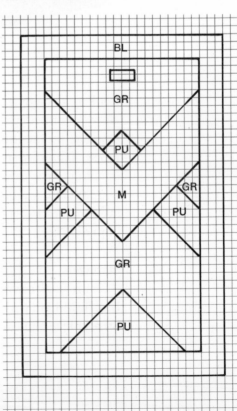

4. Block the front and back.
5. Carefully cut canvas one row away from the stitching on outside edges of the front and back.
6. Cut canvas one row away from stitching on inside rectangle on the back.
7. Overcast stitch the edges of the ends nearest the chain eyelets on the front and back pieces separately. This will leave an opening for the identification paper.
8. Overcast stitch the rectangle opening on the back.
9. Place front and back together, wrong sides facing. Overcast stitch the sides and the bottom ends together, leaving the chain end open.
10. Cut acetate or stiff plastic to fit inside tag. Slip it inside with identification paper so that name and address will be visible through the back opening.
11. Put chain through eyelet.

The back of the tag is done in the border color.

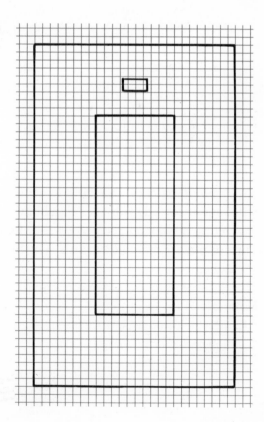

Recipe Box Patch

Needlepoint patches can be added to so many things. Overcast stitching at the edges makes finishing and fitting easy. This patch is glued to a wooden recipe box that holds 3-inch by 5-inch cards. Turn to plate 7 for color details. The finished size is 3½ inches by 5¼ inches.

Materials
#12 interlock canvas, 6½ inches by 8½ inches
Wooden recipe box

The lettering, handle, rim, and feet of the pot are dark brown.
The pot is gold. The puffs of steam are white and the background is yellow.

Yarn 33-inch lengths
- 2 dark brown
- 2 white
- 4 yellow
- 14 gold

Directions

1. Check measurements of the top of your recipe box. If it varies from this one, adjust by increasing or decreasing the background area.
2. Transfer the design to canvas, centering it so there is a 1½-inch border of canvas on all sides.
3. Stitch the design first, doing the dark brown, then the gold, and then the white. Fill in the background and block.
4. Carefully trim canvas one row away from stitching on all sides.
5. Overcast stitch the edges.
6. Glue needlepoint to the box top with fabric glue. Use pushpins or rubber bands to hold in place while the glue dries or weight down with a heavy book.

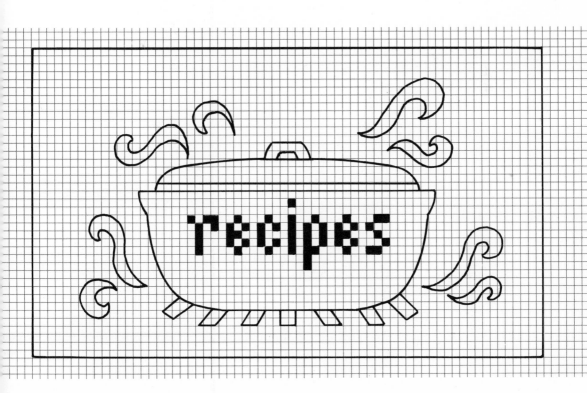

Flower Holder

A tin can that once held peanuts is now a container for flowers. Slip a small potted plant inside or a short fat glass filled with water for cut flowers. The design is pink and cream on a green background. Turn to plate 4 for color details.

Materials
#12 mono or interlock canvas, 6½ inches by 16½ inches
12-ounce nut can

Yarn   33-inch lengths
     4   pink ·
    12   cream ╱
    36   green

Directions
1. Center and draw the design outline of 3⅝ inches by 13 inches on the canvas. Adjust the measurements if necessary.

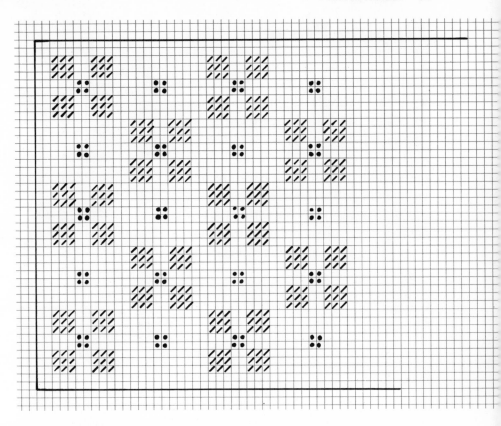

Draw a rectangle 3⅝ inches by 13 inches, or whatever size fits the can you
are using, on your canvas and continue the stitching across the width.

2. See graph for stitch design. Stitch the cream first, the pink
   second, and then fill in the background.
3. Work two extra rows on the top and bottom edges for the turnover. Check fit on the can and adjust if necessary. Block.
4. Trim canvas to ¾ of an inch from yarn edge on all sides. If mono
   canvas was used machine-stitch the canvas edge.
5. Turn canvas and two rows of stitching on the top and bottom
   edges to the back and baste. Turn canvas on ends to the back,
   leaving one row of canvas on each end exposed for joining. Baste.
6. Start at the top of the ends and whipstitch ½ of an inch down
   as shown in the photograph on page 21. Slip needlepoint over
   can and continue stitching to the bottom. Hold canvas in place
   with rubber bands while working.

Tipping Purse

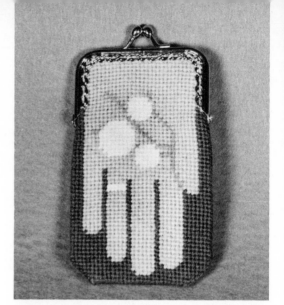

Anyone who travels will find a purse for tip money especially handy and the design on this one leaves no doubt as to what its purpose is. The metal handle has a double rim into which the finished needlepoint will be inserted. This leaves a decorative edge showing across the top of the purse. Turn to plate 3 for color details. The finished size is 3 inches by 5 inches.

Materials
#12 mono or interlock canvas,
 8 inches by 11 inches
2¾-inch handle with double-rim edge
2 pieces of lining fabric, the same
 size as needlepoint plus ½ of an
 inch allowance for seams on all
 sides

Yarn 33-inch lengths
 2 dark pink
 2 white
 10 green
 20 pink

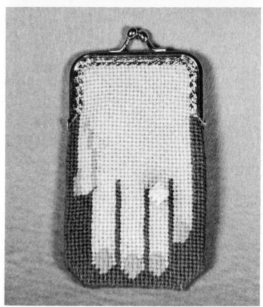

Directions
1. Transfer designs to the canvas, leaving 1½ inches between the front and back. Stain or paint the design.
2. Stitch the lines on the hands and the fingernails first, followed by the rings and the coins. Continue stitching the hands and then do the background. Block the needlepoint.
3. Trim canvas to ½ of an inch from the yarn edge. If mono canvas was used, machine-stitch the canvas edge.

The lines on the hands are dark pink; the ring, the ring band, and the coins are white. The fingernails are dark pink and the hands are pink. The background is green.

4. Turn canvas edge under on all sides. Leave one row of canvas exposed on the sides and bottom for joining. Baste.

5. Slip the wrist end of both needlepoint pieces into handle rims. Sew needlepoint to the handle with a double strand of sewing thread.

6. Whipstitch sides and bottom of both pieces together, starting just below the last sewn stitch on the handle.

7. With right sides facing, stitch sides and bottom of both lining pieces together, leaving ½ of an inch for a seam allowance. Do not turn.

8. Slip the lining into purse. Fold the top edge under and sew lining to the handle, using the same holes you used to attach the needlepoint. If your handle requires that the needlepoint be sewn to the outside edge, follow directions for the little girl purse.

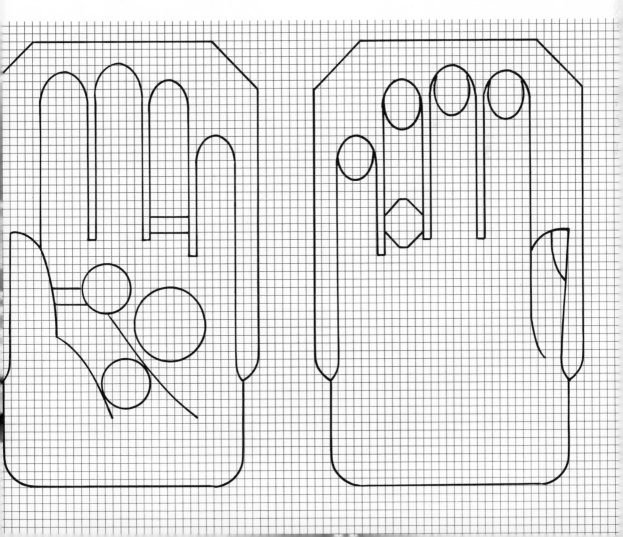

Christmas Tree Ornaments

Needlepoint ornaments add something special to a Christmas tree. A metal bell at the bottom completes the festive look and cotton stuffing rounds out the form and gives the ornaments dimension. Turn to plate 5 to see the color details. The finished size of each dome shape is 3 inches by 3¼ inches; the wreath is 3 inches round; the angel is 4 inches by 4¼ inches.

Materials

#12 mono or interlock canvas: 7 pieces, 6 inches by
    6¼ inches, for the domes and the wreath; 1 piece, 7 inches
    by 7¼ inches, for the angel (If you are clustering several
    designs on one large piece of canvas, leave 1½ inches
    between them and a 1½-inch border all around)
Felt backing cut to the ornament shape
Cotton or Dacron stuffing
Red cording for edges
Bells

Yarn   33-inch lengths

PACKAGE		CANDLE	
1	red R	6	white
1	orange OR	2	yellow Y
6	pink	1	orange OR
1	light green	2	red R
1	medium green	1	light green LT GR
1	dark green	1	dark green DK GR
		1	black

SANTA		WREATH	
5	dark green	2	red R
1	red R	1	dark pink DK P
1	blue	1	light green
1	light pink LT P	5	dark green
1	dark pink	6	white
1	cream CR		
4	white W		

(Yarn, continued)

ANGEL
- 1 yellow   Y
- 2 orange   OR
- 1 light pink
- 1 dark pink
- 2 green
- 6 white
- 10 blue

DOVE
- 3 white
- 6 blue
- 1 light green
- 1 red

HEART
- 5 pink
- 4 red
- 1 orange   OR

TREE
- 6 white
- 3 dark green
- 1 pink
- 2 red

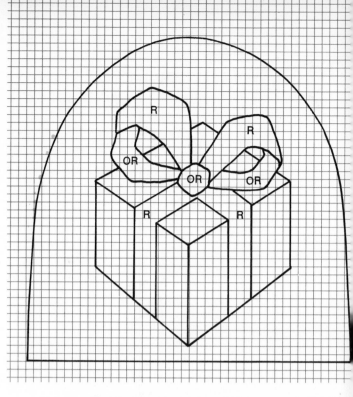

The top of the package is light green, the left-hand side is medium green, and the right-hand side is dark green. The background is pink. The ribbon is color-labeled

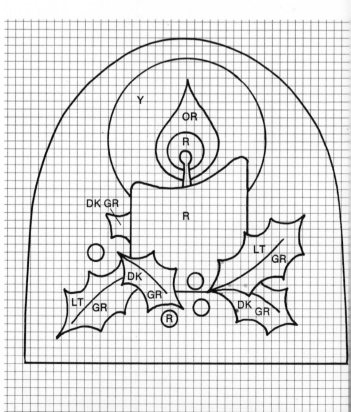

The candle and flame are color-labeled except for the wick which is black. The lines on the dark green leaves are light green and those on the light green leaves are dark green. All the berries are orange except for the single red one which is color-labeled. The background is white.

Santa Claus's mouth is red, his nose dark pink. The whites of his eyes are white and the irises are blue. The background is dark green. Everything else is color-labeled.

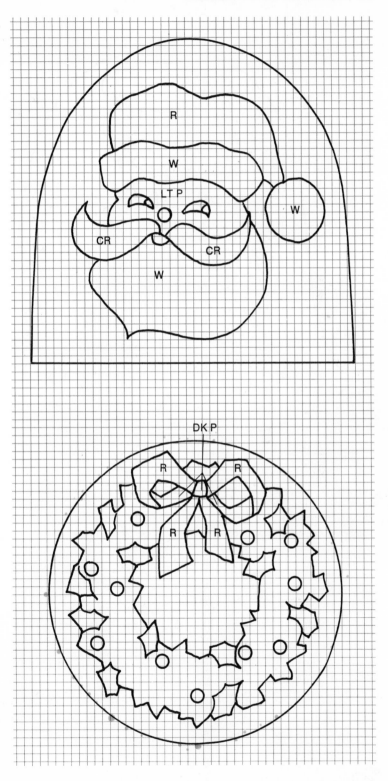

The berries on the wreath are done alternately in dark pink and red. The main body of the wreath is dark green and the small sections on the inside and outside of the wreath are light green. The ribbon is color-labeled and the background is white.

The angel's face and hands are light pink. The mouth is dark pink and the eyes are blue. The border of the white robe is green and the little dots between the scallops are dark pink. The yellow halo and the orange hair are color-labeled. The background is blue. (Designed by Jean Ray Laury)

Directions

1. Transfer designs to the canvas and stain or paint.
2. Stitch designs beginning with the smallest elements. Block the needlepoint.
3. Trim canvas ½ of an inch from yarn edge. If mono canvas was used, machine-stitch canvas edge.
4. Turn canvas edge to the back and baste in place.
5. Blindstitch the cording around the edge. Attach a yarn loop at the top of the ornament and attach a bell at the bottom; the

The dove is white on a blue background. The berries and the dove's eye are red. The leaves above the dove are light green.

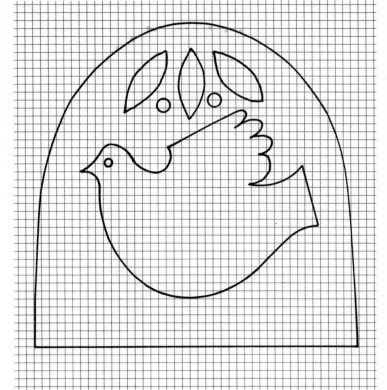

The heart is red on a background of pink. The orange details are color-labeled.

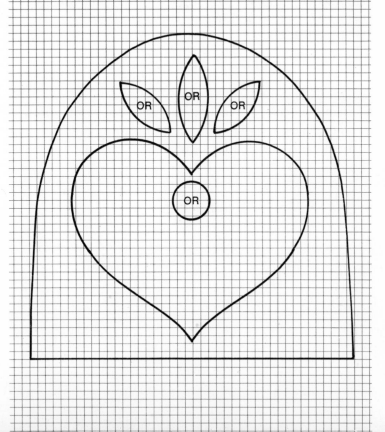

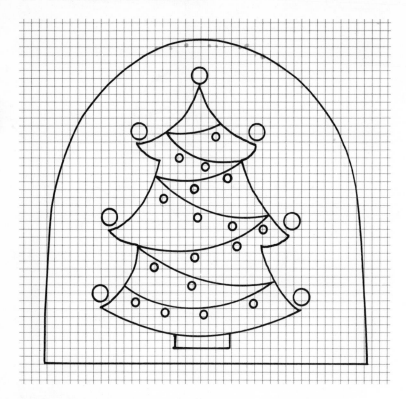

The Christmas tree is dark green and the ornaments at the tips of the boughs are red. The garland is red and the ornaments on the garland and the treetop are dark pink. The base of the tree is red and the background is white.

wreath does not have a bell and the angel does not have cording.

6. Turn the ornament facedown. Place a layer of cotton or Dacron on the back and place a piece of felt over it. Blindstitch the felt to the canvas at the cording edge.

Hatband

The flower design on this hatband can also be used to decorate a belt or trim a window shade. The finished size of the hatband in the photograph is 1 inch by 28 inches. To determine the length for your band, measure your hat around the base of the crown and add 6 inches for a crossover of the ends. Turn to plate 4 for color details.

Materials
#12 interlock canvas, 4 inches by 31 inches
Grosgrain ribbon, 1 inch by 29 inches

Yarn   33-inch lengths
   2   yellow ✕
   6   white •
 16   blue (background)
 10   green (border)

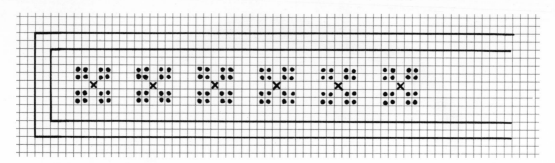

Continue this stitching for the length of the band.

Directions

1. Draw the design outline (13 stitches wide, 28 inches long) onto canvas, centering it to leave even edges of canvas. Adjust the length if necessary.
2. Follow the design on the graph, stitching flowers first. The yellow centers are cross-stitched, as shown on page 17.
3. Stitch the blue background and one row of the green border. Leave the outside row on all edges unstitched. Block the needlepoint.
4. Carefully cut canvas on row away from yarn edge.
5. Overcast stitch the edges and ends with green yarn.
6. To line the back with grosgrain ribbon, turn the ends of the ribbon under ½ of an inch and blindstitch to the ends of the bands; ribbon edges are already finished and do not need to be turned. Blindstitch ribbon to sides of needlepoint.
7. Tack band to hat at the place where the band crosses over itself.

Brick
Bookends

The size and weight of bricks make them ideal to use as bookends. There are six sides of each brick to cover. This brick is covered with needlepoint on four sides (the ones that show) and with felt on two sides. Turn to plate 11 to see the bookend in color. The finished size is 8 inches by 3¾ inches by 2½ inches.

Materials
#12 mono or interlock canvas, 9½ inches by 16 inches
Brick
Felt

Yarn   33-inch lengths
    8   red brown
  20   cream
  12   black
  32   red

Directions
1. Transfer the design to the canvas. Adjust size to the exact measurement of the brick by increasing or decreasing the background color. Paint or stain the design.
2. Following the graph, stitch the design and then block.

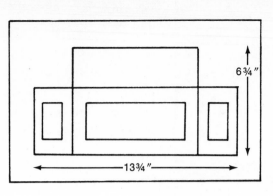

Placing the pattern on the canvas

The bookend design. The background is stitched in red, while the panel for the lettering is cream and the lettering itself is red brown. The panels on the ends of the brick are cream and the border is black.

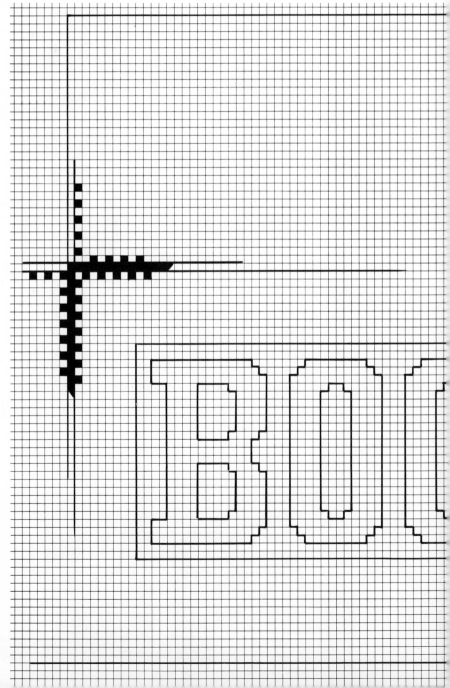

3. Trim canvas to 1 inch from the yarn edge. If mono canvas was used, machine-stitch the canvas edge.

4. With a whipstitch, join the top edge of one end panel to side of the top panel, as shown in the second photograph on the following page. Trim the top edge of each end panel and the two sides

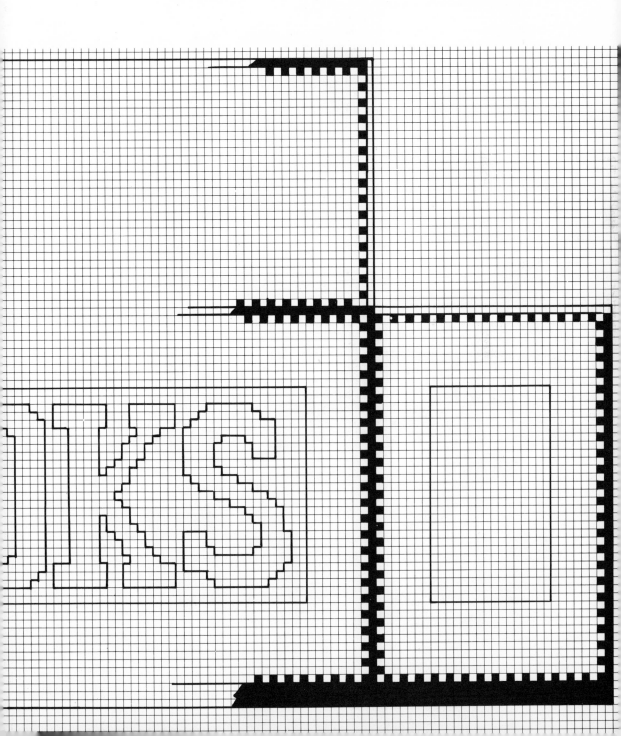

Detail of the border

of the top panel to ½ of an inch from the yarn before joining. Repeat at the other end.

5. Fit needlepoint on the brick and secure with rubber bands. Fold the canvas corners to lie flat.

6. Lace the canvas in two directions—vertically and horizontally— as shown on page 22.

7. Cut one piece of felt to cover the lacing over brick. Blindstitch the felt to yarn at the edges.

Whipstitching the end to the top

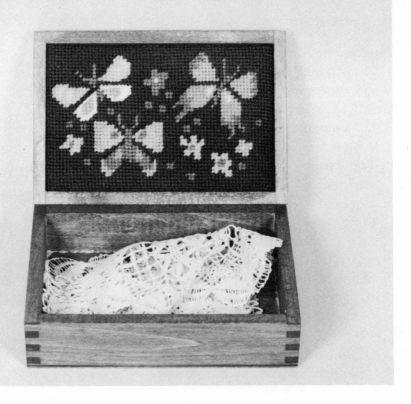

Catchall Box

It is a pleasant surprise to open a box and discover a splash of needlepoint color inside. These wooden boxes are available in hobby shops. The finished size of the needlepoint is 3½ inches by 5½ inches, which fits a standard box. Turn to plate 2 for the color scheme.

Materials
#12 mono or interlock canvas, 6½ inches by 8½ inches
Wooden box
Cardboard

Yarn 33-inch lengths

2	light orange	LT OR	1	yellow Y
1	orange OR		1	light blue
2	pink P		1	light green
2	dark pink DK P		14	dark blue

Directions

1. Transfer the design to the canvas. If necessary, adjust size to exact measurement of box lid inset. Paint or stain the design.
2. Stitch the design and block.
3. Cut a piece of cardboard ⅛ of an inch smaller than the stitched design.
4. Trim canvas to ¾ of an inch from yarn edge. If mono canvas was used, machine-stitch the canvas edge.
5. Lay needlepoint facedown and place cardboard over it. Fold canvas edges over the cardboard, fold canvas flat at the corners.
6. Lace the needlepoint in place, as shown in the photograph on page 22.
7. Slip needlepoint into the inset of the box lid. The fit should be tight enough to keep needlepoint in place. If it is not, glue the needlepoint to the inside of the lid.

The flower at the top is dark pink with a yellow center. The smaller flower at the lower right is pink with a yellow center. The other flowers are light orange with dark pink centers. All of the scattered dots are light green and the background is dark blue. The three butterflies have light blue antennas and bodies. Abbreviations give the colors for the wings; the opposite wings are identical.

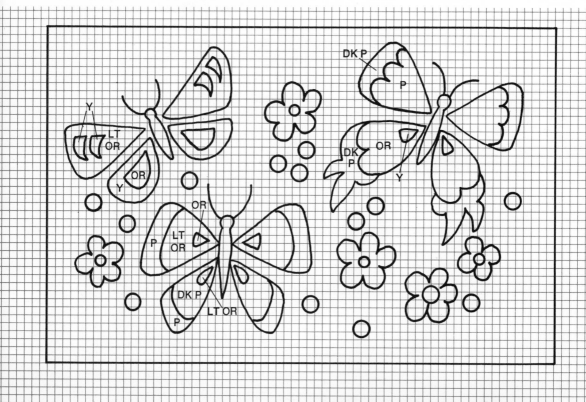

Coasters

Coasters are small, easy to stitch, and make nice gifts. These house coasters would be especially welcomed as a housewarming present. For other designs that adapt well for coasters, see the sachet holders and the candleholder base. Each of these is a 3-inch-square design; to increase them to coaster size add 2 rows of border color. The finished size of each coaster is 3¼ inches by 3¼ inches. Turn to plate 7 for the color details.

Materials
#12 mono or interlock canvas, 6 inches by 6 inches for
    each coaster (If you are clustering several designs

on one large piece of canvas, leave 1½ inches between
them and a 1½-inch border all around)
Felt for each coaster

Yarn   33-inch lengths

YELLOW HOUSE

1   yellow   Y
1   dark yellow   DK Y
2   medium brown   MED BR
1   light brown
3   blue
3   white   W
1   dark green
3   olive

RED HOUSE

1   red   R
2   dark red   DK R
3   blue
1   light brown
1   dark green
3   white   W
3   olive

GREEN HOUSE

1   green   GR
1   dark green   DK GR
1   red
1   orange
2   white
2   medium brown   MED BR
1   dark brown
1   light brown
2   blue
3   olive

BROWN HOUSE

2   light brown   LT BR
1   medium brown   MED BR
1   dark brown
1   dark yellow
1   orange
4   white   W
4   blue
3   olive

Directions
1. Transfer designs to canvas and stain or paint.
2. Stitch design and block.
3. Trim canvas to ½ of an inch from the yarn edge. If mono canvas
   was used, machine-stitch the canvas edge. Turn canvas and one
   row of stitching on all edges to the back and baste. If you are
   using interlock canvas, finish the edge with an overcast stitch.
4. Place felt over back of canvas. Pin and blindstitch felt to yarn
   edge. A 3-inch square of flexible plastic can be inserted between
   canvas and felt to keep moisture from felt.

All the coasters are winter scenes and the snow on the ground is white, the sky blue, and the clouds white. All the pathways are light brown and the borders are olive. The rest of the color schemes are given with each design.

Yellow house.
The snow-laden tree is dark green as is the door. The doorknob is dark yellow and all the windows are light brown. The rest of the features are color-labeled on the design.

Red house.
The dark green door has a red doorknob. All the windows are light brown. The walls, chimney, and snow-covered roof are color-labeled.

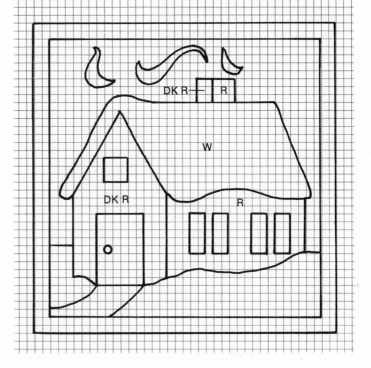

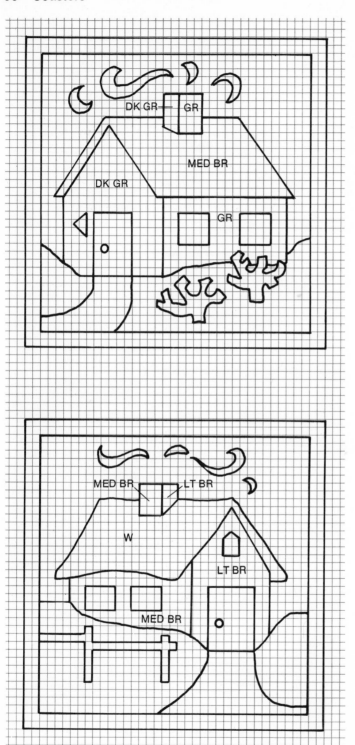

Green house.
The red door has a dark green doorknob and all the windows are orange. The leafless shrubbery is dark brown. The walls, roof, and chimney are color-labeled.

Brown house.
The orange door has a medium brown doorknob. All the windows are dark yellow and the fence is dark brown. The walls, chimney, and snow-covered roof are color-labeled.

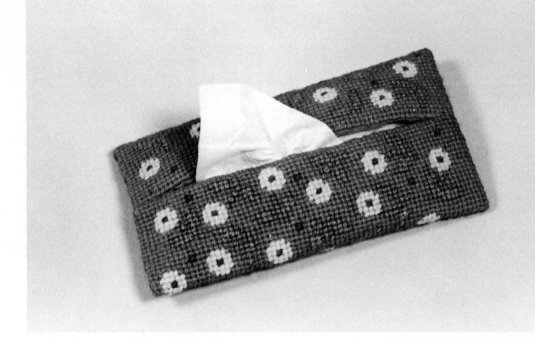

Kleenex Case

Cover a purse-sized kleenex package with needlepoint and you have
a pretty container for your handbag. This design, inspired by a
provincial print, scatters yellow flowers at random. The flowers
are all stitched by the graph. The blue centers and dots are cross-
stitched. The green leaves and stems and the red background are
stitched in the usual way. Turn to plate 6 for the color details. The
finished size is 3¼ inches by 5¾ inches.

Materials
#12 mono or interlock canvas, 9 inches by 9¾ inches
Lining fabric, 7 inches by 7¾ inches

Yarn   33-inch lengths
  6   yellow
  8   green
  2   blue
  30   red (background)

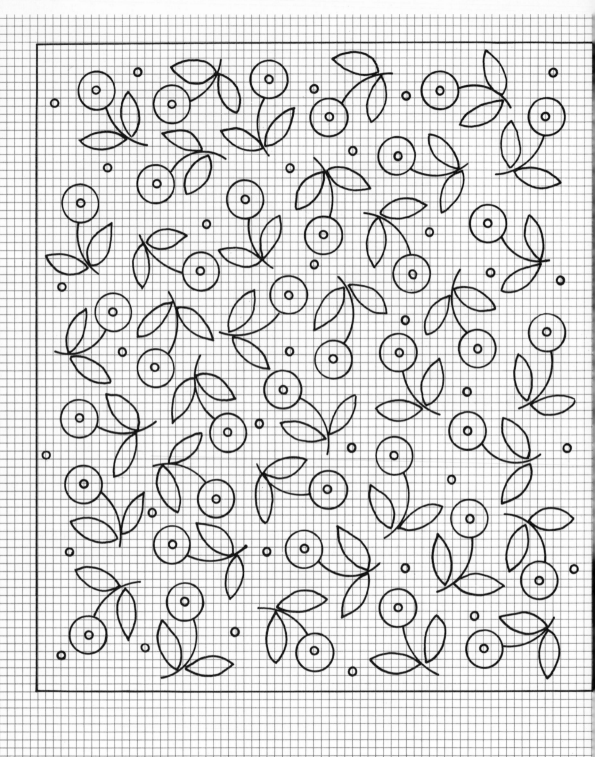

The kleenex case design

Graph for
the flowers

Directions

1. Transfer design to canvas, centering it to leave even amounts of canvas on the sides. Stain or paint the design.
2. Following the graph, stitch yellow flowers first. Cross-stitch the blue centers and dots, stitch the stems and leaves, and then fill in the background. Block the needlepoint.
3. Trim canvas to ½ of an inch from yarn edge. If mono canvas was used, machine-stitch the canvas edge.
4. Turn the canvas and one row of stitching under on the 6-inch ends. Baste.
5. Turn the canvas edge under on the 6¾-inch sides, leaving one row of canvas exposed for joining. Baste.
6. While the canvas is flat, fit the lining to the inside. Turn lining edges under ½ of an inch and blindstitch in place. Stitch lining to yarn at the 6-inch ends. On the 6¾-inch sides be sure to leave the one row of canvas exposed for joining.
7. Find the center point of each side. Fold the ends to meet at center point, as shown in the first drawing.
8. Whipstitch the sides together. With hidden stitches, sew opening together ¼ of an inch in from each side, as in the drawing.

Folding the ends
to meet the center point

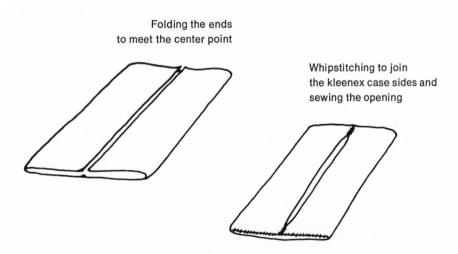

Whipstitching to join
the kleenex case sides and
sewing the opening

Sachet Holders

The delicate fragrance of a sachet is refreshing when one opens a drawer or closet door. You can make these sachet holders into small pillows that will nestle in a drawer or you can add a loop and hang them in a closet over a clothes hanger. If you wish, the designs can be used as squares for coasters. Turn to plate 9 for color details. The finished size of each sachet is 3 inches by 3 inches.

Materials
#12 mono or interlock canvas, 6 inches by 6 inches each
    (If you are clustering several designs on one piece of
    canvas, leave 1 ½ inches between designs and a 1 ½-inch
    border all around)
Backing fabric
Sachet fragrance

Cotton batting
Yarn for loop and tassels

Yarn   33-inch lengths

DAISIES

2   white
1   yellow
1   green   GR
1   dark green   DK GR
6   blue

SCATTERED FLOWERS

1   lavender
1   purple
1   yellow
1   dark pink
1   pink
1   green
5   bone

RED FLORAL

1   coral
2   red
1   dark red
1   light green   LT GR
2   dark green   DK GR
5   chocolate brown

RIBBON-TIED BOUQUET

1   light pink
1   medium pink
1   dark pink
2   dark green
1   light green
1   blue
6   ecru

Daisies. The top daisy is yellow with a white center, the one to the right is white, the one to the bottom is yellow, and the fourth daisy is white with a yellow center. The dark green or green leaves and stems are labeled, and the background is blue.

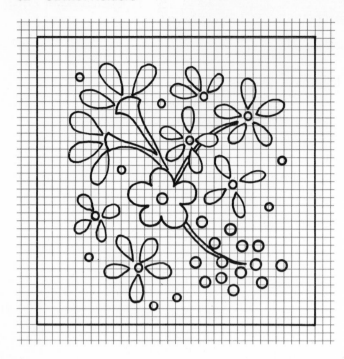

Scattered flowers. The center flower is dark pink, while the two flowers at the top left are pink; the three flowers at the top right and the one at the bottom are lavender, and the two flowers on either side of the central dark pink flower are purple. All flower centers are yellow and the stems are green. The dots are alternately pink and dark pink with a few purple ones, as shown in plate 9. The background is bone.

Red floral. The center of the large flower is dark red, surrounded by coral and then red. The bottom flower is red with a dark green stem, and the flower at the left is coral with a red base and a dark green stem. The leaves are labeled as light green and dark green. The small dots are coral and the background is chocolate brown.

Ribbon-tied bouquet. All the stems are dark green and all the leaves are light green. The colors of the flowers, which are dark pink, medium pink, and light pink, are randomly distributed in almost equal amounts as shown in plate 9. The ribbon is blue and the background is ecru.

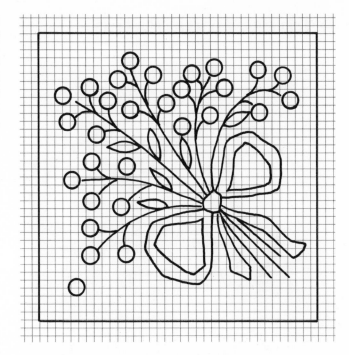

Directions

1. Transfer the design to the canvas and stain or paint.
2. Stitch design. The small dots are cross-stitched, as shown in the drawing on page 17. Block the needlepoint.
3. Trim canvas to ½ of an inch from yarn edge. If mono canvas was used, machine-stitch the canvas edge.
4. Cut backing fabric to fit the design, adding a ½-inch seam allowance.
5. Place the needlepoint and the backing fabric together, right sides facing, and baste at the edges on three sides. Machine-stitch together at the yarn edge.
6. Remove the basting and turn right side out.
7. Make a pillow form with two pieces of lightweight cotton batting and place the sachet filling in the center.
8. Slip the pillow into the needlepoint case. Turn the edges of the open side under and blindstitch the backing fabric to the yarn edge.
9. If you wish, attach a loop of yarn at one corner to make a hanger and a tassel at the opposite corner. See the drawings on page 24.

Address Book Patch

Dress up an address book with a patch. This patch is glued to a 4-inch by 5¼-inch address book purchased at a stationery store. The same patch with different lettering is very effective on a telephone book cover. Turn to plate 1 for color details.

Materials
#12 interlock canvas, 7 inches by 8½ inches
Address book

Yarn 33-inch lengths

2	dark blue	2	dark yellow
1	light green	4	cream
3	green	10	light blue
1	yellow		

1. Candleholder base, address book patch, and jewelry case

2. Catchall box

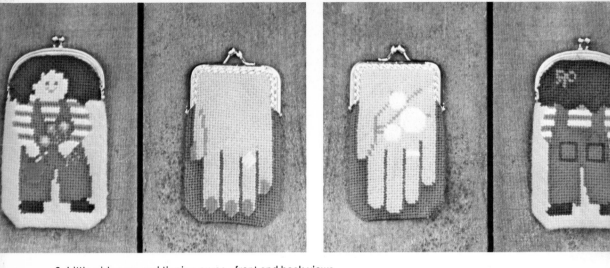

3. Little girl purse and tipping purse—front and back views

4. Hatband and flower holder

5. Christmas tree ornaments

6. Black and white purse
and kleenex case

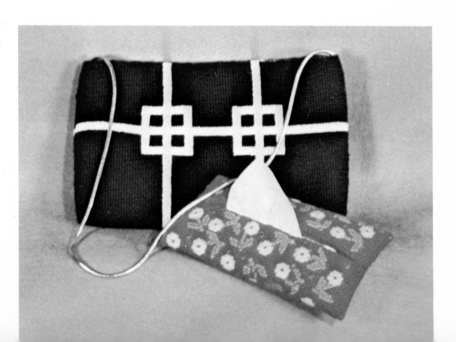

7. Recipe box patch and coasters

8. Multistriped purse

9. Sachet holders

10. Wedding photo album

11. Brick bookends

12. Desk set—pencil holder, calendar frame,
    and mirror frame

13. Floral purse

14. Travel makeup case

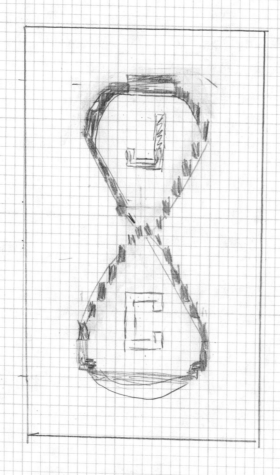

15. Sunny day bank, hosiery travel case, and sewing kit

16. Hearts set—contact-lens case, purse, and manicure case

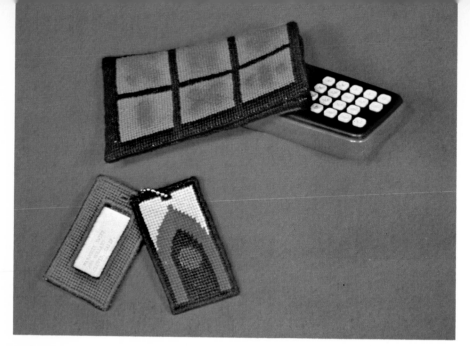

17. Hand-calculator case and luggage tags

18. Sewing box and camera case with strap

Directions

1. Transfer design to the center of the canvas. Stain or paint the design.
2. Stitch design, beginning with the lettering and the smaller details and ending with the background. Then block the needlepoint.
3. Carefully cut canvas one row away from stitching on all edges.
4. Overcast stitch the edges, changing color when necessary to continue the design.
5. Use fabric glue to attach needlepoint patch to the front of the address book, and weight down with a heavy book.

The lettering, the roof lines, and the tree trunk are dark blue. The houses are cream with dark yellow windows and doors. The sun is yellow and the top of the tree is light green. The strip of grass at the bottom and the band behind the lettering are green. The background is light blue.

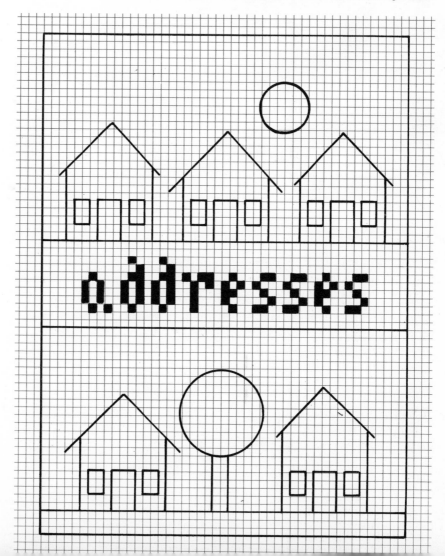

Sewing Box

This wooden box helps to organize sewing supplies, and has a pincushion top. Craft shops have different sizes of wooden boxes with inset lids. A box with an inset of about ½ of an inch provides a nice depth for a pincushion. Stain or paint the box to blend with the yarn colors. Turn to plate 18 for color details. The finished size of this pincushion top is 4½ inches by 6 inches.

Materials
#12 mono or interlock canvas, 7½ inches by 9 inches
Wooden box with inset lid
Cardboard to fit inset
Cotton batting

Yarn 33-inch lengths

3	orange	2	light green LT GR
2	pink P	3	green GR
1	red	1	light blue LT BL
2	white	2	yellow
1	lavender	22	dark blue

Directions

1. Use the measurement of the box top inset for the size of the pincushion outline. Draw the outline on canvas and transfer the

The large center flower is orange with red markings and a pink center. The top left flower is yellow with orange markings and a red center. The two daisies at the top are white with yellow centers and the other daisy is yellow with a white center. All the three-petaled flowers are pink with orange at the base of the petals. The small dots without labels are all lavender and the background is dark blue. The leaves, the large dot beneath the central flower, and the rest of the small dots are color-labeled.

pattern. Make any necessary adjustments in size by increasing or decreasing the background. Stain or paint the design.

2. Stitch design beginning with the smallest parts. Add two rows of background color on all edges. Block.

3. Trim canvas to ¾ of an inch from yarn edge. If you have used mono canvas, machine-stitch canvas edge.

4. Cut the cardboard ³⁄₁₆ of an inch smaller than the inset opening.

5. Glue a 1½-inch-thick layer of cotton batting to the top of the cardboard. Be sure to use cotton batting, since Dacron batting will rust your needles.

6. Center the needlepoint over your padded top and fold edges over to the back of the cardboard. Fold canvas flat at the corners.

7. Lace in place as shown on page 22. The padded top should fit snugly in the inset. If it does not, glue it to the lid.

Desk Set—Pencil Holder, Mirror Frame, and Calendar Frame

A pencil holder, calendar frame, and mirror frame make up this desk set; the mirror enables a busy woman to make a quick check before an appointment. It's quite easy to put all this together. The pencil holder is made from a tin can, the mirror is slipped into a picture frame, and the small calendar is glued to a cardboard backing, then each piece is covered or framed with a geometric needlepoint design. Turn to plate 12 for color details. The finished size of the pencil holder is 4½ inches tall; both the mirror and the calendar frame are 4 inches by 5 inches.

Pencil Holder

Materials

#12 interlock canvas, 7 ½ inches by 13 inches

15-ounce tin can

Yarn   33-inch lengths

    6   red •

    8   straw-colored \

    8   gold /

  26   dark red (background)

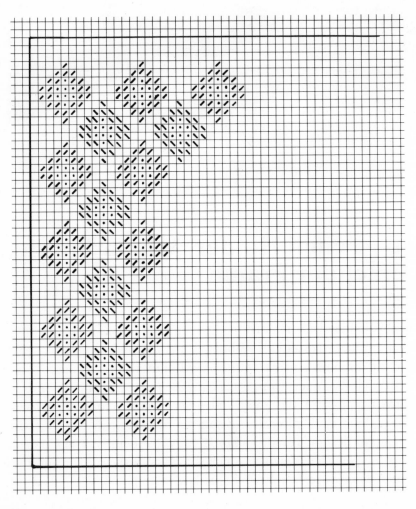

Pencil holder design. Draw the outline 4½ inches by 10 inches, or whatever size will fit the tin can you are using. Continue the design across the canvas.

Directions

1. Measure the height and circumference of the can and use these measurements for the outline of your pattern. Draw the outline on canvas. Yarn calculations for this design were based on a can that measured 4½ inches tall and 10 inches around.

2. See the graph for stitch design. Start the first line of the design on the fourth row from top edge. Fill in the rectangle with the design.

3. Stitch background, leaving one row on the top and bottom edges unstitched for the overcast stitch. Check the fit over the can and adjust if necessary. Block.

4. Carefully trim canvas one row away from the yarn stitching at the top and bottom edges. Trim canvas to ½ of an inch from yarn edge on each end.

5. Overcast stitch the top and bottom edges with the background color.

6. Turn canvas under at each end, leaving one row of canvas exposed for joining. Baste.

7. Spray-paint the inside of the can with dark-colored paint or line the insides with felt.

8. Starting at the top of the ends, whipstitch ½ of an inch down with dark red yarn. Slip needlepoint over can and continue stitching to the bottom. Use rubber bands to hold needlepoint in place while you are working, as shown on page 21.

Mirror Frame

Materials

#12 interlock canvas, 7 inches by 8 inches
Picture frame, 4 inches by 4 inches, for tabletop
Mirror, 2¼ inches by 2¾ inches

Yarn   33-inch lengths
- 2   red ·
- 4   straw-colored \
- 4   gold /
- 7   dark red (background)

Design for
the calendar and
mirror frame

Directions
1. Draw the outside edge and the mirror outline on the canvas.
2. Stitch one row of dark red one row away from outside edge and one row away from the mirror edge.
3. See the graph for stitch design. Work design, leaving one row on the outside and mirror edge unstitched. Block.
4. Carefully trim the canvas one row from the yarn stitching on outside. Cut the inside edge as in the photograph.
5. Overcast stitch the edges with dark red yarn.

6. Place the needlepoint and the mirror on the cardboard backing that comes with the picture frame. Glue in place with fabric glue and slip into the frame.

Calendar Frame

Materials
#12 interlock canvas, 7 inches by 8 inches
Cardboard for backing and easel hinge
Calendar

Cutting the inside edge for the mirror or calendar

Yarn   33-inch lengths

   3   red ·

   4   straw-colored \

   4   gold ╱

  10   dark red (background)

Directions

1. Draw the outside edge and calendar outline on the canvas. If your calendar is a different size than this one, draw the outline in the center of the canvas and adjust your design around it.
2. Follow steps 2 through 5 of the mirror frame directions.
3. Cut cardboard backing to fit the needlepoint and using fabric glue, attach needlepoint and calendar to the cardboard.
4. Make the cardboard stand and glue it to the center back of the cardboard as shown in the drawings.

Full-size pattern for the cardboard easel hinge

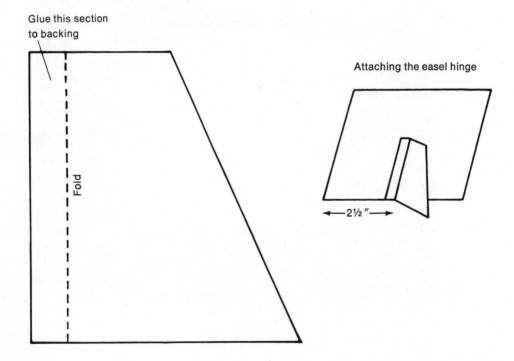

Glue this section to backing

Fold

Attaching the easel hinge

←—2½ "—→

 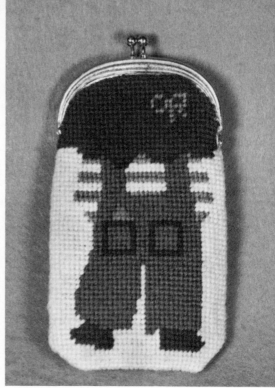

Little Girl Purse

This purse makes a charming gift for a little girl. To add a more personal touch, you will probably want to change the hair color and some of the other details to match those of the recipient. The needlepoint purse is easily attached to a curved purse handle. Turn to plate 3 for color details. The finished size is 3¼ inches by 5 inches.

Materials
#12 mono or interlock canvas, 8 inches by 12 inches
3-inch curved purse frame designed to be sewn on the outside
2 pieces of lining fabric, 4 inches by 6 inches each

Yarn   33-inch lengths

2	light pink	2	green
1	dark pink	10	yellow
1	red	10	dark brown
2	white	10	blue

Directions

1. Transfer the designs to the canvas. Both front and back can be placed on the same piece of canvas; leave a 1½-inch border all around and 1½ inches between designs. Stain or paint the designs.
2. Stitch the designs, starting with the smallest elements. Then block the needlepoint.
3. Trim canvas to ½ of an inch from the yarn edge. If mono canvas was used, machine-stitch the canvas edge.

4. Turn the curved end of both pieces of needlepoint so that one row of stitches folds over the back, then baste.
5. Turn the canvas edges of sides and bottoms under, leaving one row of canvas exposed for joining. Baste.
6. Sew the curved ends of both pieces to the handle, using sewing thread to match the hair color.
7. Whipstitch sides and bottom of front and back pieces together, starting just below the last sewn stitch on the handle.
8. With right sides facing, sew the sides and bottom of the two

The little girl has dark brown hair; her eyes are blue, her mouth is dark pink, and her face and hands are light pink. The dark pink flowers she carries have yellow centers and green stems. The bucket is red and the spade handle in the bucket is yellow. Her shirt is green and white striped, her overalls are blue, and her shoes are dark brown. On the back view, she wears a green hair ribbon; the pockets are outlined in dark brown and there is a red handkerchief in one pocket.

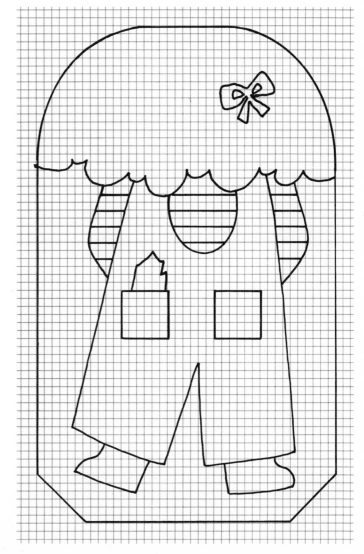

pieces of lining together, leaving ½ of an inch for the seam. Do not turn right side out.

9. Slip the lining into purse. Fold the top edge under, following the curved shape, sew lining to the handle, using the same holes you used for attaching the needlepoint.

Sunny Day Bank

The old adage of saving for a rainy day may be good economics, but it's not as much fun as saving for a sunny day at the beach, ski slopes, or mountain lake. There are many kinds of containers that would make good forms for savings banks. The best ones are those that have some kind of lid or opening so that you'll have access to the coins at the bottom. Cans that hold spices, dry cheese, and paint have this kind of lid. The one used here is a one-pint can. You can get these cans, clean and unused, at any store that mixes paint to order; just be sure that the end opposite the lid can be opened with a can opener. Turn to plate 15 to see color details of the bank. The finished size is 4 inches tall and 3½ inches wide.

Design for the side panel.
The background is blue,
the lettering yellow, and
the border at the bottom is
medium green. The other design
elements are color-labeled.

Materials

#12 interlock canvas: 1 piece, 7 inches by 14 inches, for
      side; 1 piece, 6½ inches by 6½ inches, for top
1-pint paint can
Cardboard and string

Yarn   33-inch lengths

6	yellow Y	1	orange OR
2	light green LT GR	2	light pink LT P
6	medium green MED GR	2	pink P
2	dark green DK GR	1	purple PU
2	olive OL	2	white W
1	gold GD	30	blue

Directions

1. Transfer the designs to canvas. Stain or paint the designs.

Design for the top of the bank. The center is yellow and the border is blue with yellow rays.

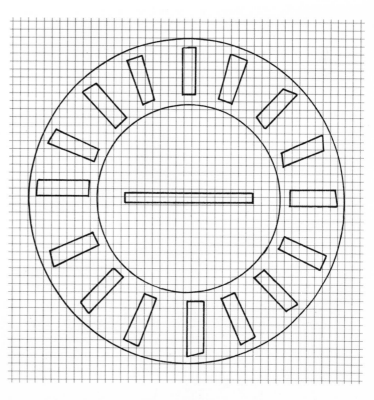

2. Stitch the design on the side panel, leaving one row unstitched at the top and bottom edges for overcast stitching.

3. Cut the coin slot in top section. With yellow yarn, stitch one row away from this cut edge, then overcast stitch the row of canvas on the slot edge. Stitch the rest of design on top section, adding two rows of stitching outside the circle edge.

4. Block both the top and side panels.

5. Remove the bottom of the can with a can opener.

6. Cut a cardboard circle to fit the bottom opening, then cut a slot in the cardboard circle to fit under the slot in the canvas. The cut in the cardboard should be a bit larger than the cut in the canvas so that the cardboard will not be visible when canvas is over it.

7. Use fabric glue to attach cardboard circle to the back of needle-point top, matching the openings in each.

8. Turn the can over so that the bottom is now the top. Glue a circle of cord or string, just inside the rim of the can. This will keep the cardboard form from slipping into the can.

9. Trim canvas 1 inch away from yarn edge on top piece. Make V-shaped cuts in the canvas edge so that canvas will fit smoothly, as shown in the drawing.

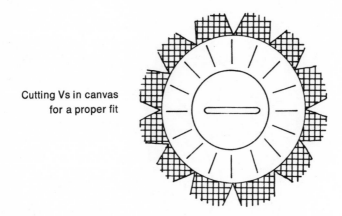

Cutting Vs in canvas
for a proper fit

10. Place the needlepoint top on the can opening, and fold the canvas edges over the outside of the can. Glue edges to sides with fabric glue, hold in place with rubber bands until dry.

11. Carefully cut canvas one row away from the yarn on the top

and bottom edges of the side panel. Trim canvas to ½ of an inch from the yarn stitching on the ends of the side panel.

12. Overcast stitch the top and bottom edges.
13. Turn the canvas of end edge to the back and baste, leaving one row of canvas on each end exposed for joining.
14. Start at top of the ends and whipstitch ½ of an inch down. Slip needlepoint over can and continue stitching to the bottom. Hold canvas in place with rubber bands while stitching.

Another side of the sunny day bank

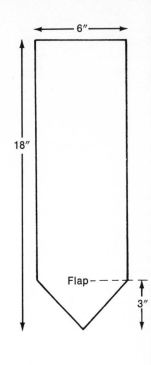

Multistriped Purse

This effective, striped purse made by LaMina Smith was originally designed to use up leftover yarn pieces. Another idea is to stitch six-row color groupings, with a light, medium, and dark shade of each color. You can either follow the colors given in the caption for the design or stitch random colors as she did. For her color scheme turn to plate 8. The finished size of the purse is 5½ inches by 6¾ inches.

Materials
#12 mono or interlock canvas, 9 inches by 22 inches

36-inch cord for shoulder strap

Velcro dot or pair of snaps

Lining fabric, the same size as needlepoint plus ½ of an inch all around for seam

Draw the design according to these dimensions, centering it on the canvas. You can follow the shape of the flap in the full-size stitching pattern.

Start stitching two rows below the flap edge with two extra rows of light yellow or whatever color you are using for the turnover. Continue with two more rows of light yellow, two rows of medium yellow, and then two rows of dark yellow. Change to blue, starting with two rows of light blue, two rows of medium blue, and two rows of dark blue. Continue in this way through green, pink, gold, turquoise, lime, rose, and back to yellow again. Repeat the same color sequence for the entire length of the purse.

Yarn 33-inch lengths
Approximately 120 strands of different colors or 5 strands of light, medium, and dark shades of the following colors: yellow, rose, lime, turquoise, gold, pink, green, and blue

Directions

1. Center and draw design outline on the canvas as shown in the drawing. The flap design is full-scale.
2. Start stitching the bottom row of the triangular flap. The stripes here

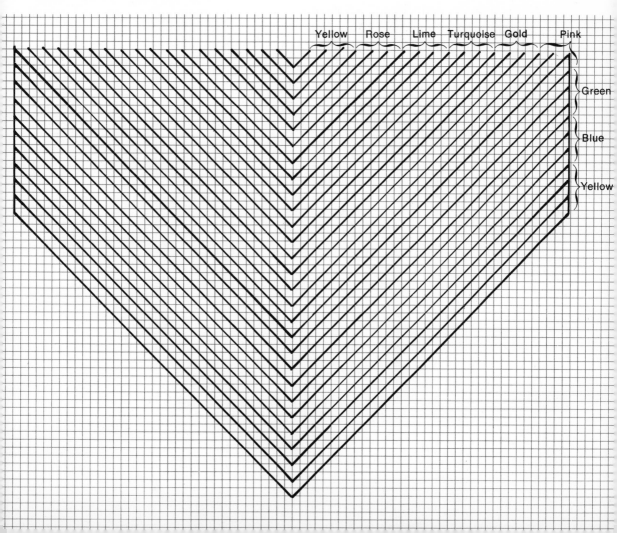

are three shades of one color, each two rows wide, totaling six rows of each color. Stitch two extra matching rows, right below triangular flap for turnover.

3. The right half of the canvas is done in the regular continental stitch, the left half is done in the continental stitch reversed to slant to the left. If you choose to work this way, it is easiest if you turn the canvas to a ¼-turn counterclockwise when stitching the left side. If you prefer, you can work the whole design with the regular continental stitch. This would mean however, that the left side would have a stair-step look, rather than the smooth look it has here.

4. Block the needlepoint and then trim canvas to ½ of an inch from the yarn edge. If mono canvas was used, machine-stitch the canvas edge.

5. With right sides together, fold the bottom of the needlepoint up 6¾ inches. Baste and machine-stitch the sides together, two rows inside the yarn edge. Turn right side out.

6. Turn the canvas plus two rows of stitching under on the flap end and baste. Turn the canvas edge of the straight end under, baste.

7. Tack the ends of the shoulder-strap cord inside the purse at top of each side seam.

8. Sew the lining as you did the needlepoint, right sides together, with a ½ of an inch seam allowance.

9. Without turning, slip the lining into the purse. Turn the flap end and the straight end under and blindstitch to the yarn edge.

10. If you wish to close purse, use snaps or Velcro dots at the flap point.

Hosiery Travel Case

Place this sunburst travel case in a suitcase or dresser drawer; it holds, protects, and helps you to keep track of stockings. The inset is made of a synthetic suede fabric; since it requires no turning under of edges, a zipper is easily sewn in place. Turn to plate 15 for color details. The finished size is 5 inches by 6 inches by 1½ inches and there's plenty of room for several pairs.

Materials
#12 mono or interlock canvas, 9 inches by 14 inches
Side inset fabric, 2½ inches by 13½ inches (to match or
    harmonize with the border)
12-inch zipper
2 pieces of lining fabric, the same size as needlepoint
    plus ½ of an inch all around for seam

Yarn   33-inch lengths

5	light pink LT P		4	gold GD
3	medium pink MED P		4	dark gold DK GD
5	light yellow LT Y		8	orange OR
4	medium yellow MED Y		6	burnt orange BU OR
5	dark yellow DK Y			(plus 8 for border)

Directions

1. Transfer the design to center of the canvas. Stain or paint the design.

Design for hosiery travel case

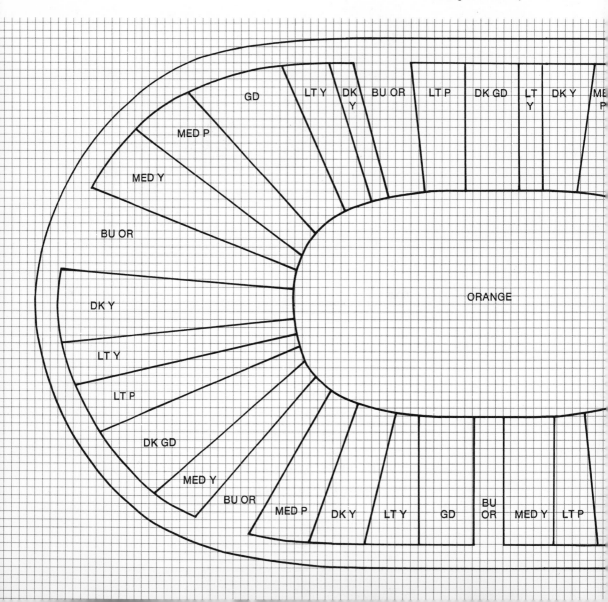

2. Stitch the design, starting at the center oval. Choose one of the ray colors for the border color; the one used here is burnt orange. It takes eight pieces of yarn to make the border. Block the needlepoint.
3. Trim the canvas to ½ of an inch from the yarn edge. If mono canvas was used, machine-stitch the canvas edge.
4. To add the zipper, make a 12-inch-long cut, ⅞ of an inch away from one side of the inset fabric; be sure to leave an equal amount of fabric at either end of the zipper. Trim the cut so that it is ⅛ of an inch wide, as shown in the drawing.

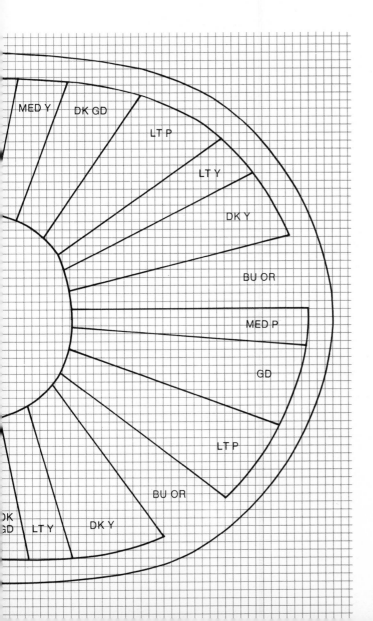

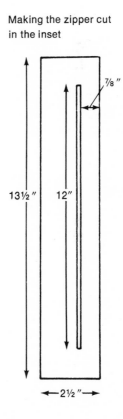

Making the zipper cut in the inset

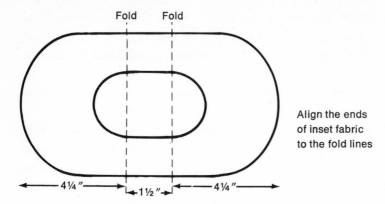

Align the ends
of inset fabric
to the fold lines

5. Sew in the zipper without turning under the edges of the opening.
6. Pin the inset fabric to the needlepoint with right sides together.
Match ends of fabric to the fold lines on the needlepoint. Baste
and then machine-stitch, leaving a ½-inch seam allowance. Clip
corners if necessary; leave the zipper partially open for turning
right side out.
7. Cut the lining the same as needlepoint pattern plus ½ of an inch
seam allowance.
8. Fold edges of lining fabric under ½ of an inch and blindstitch to
wrong side of needlepoint. Do not line inset section. Then turn.

Hand-Calculator Case

Calculators have become such a part of our everyday lives, it is convenient to keep one in an easily identifiable needlepoint case. This one incorporates mathematical symbols in the design. Turn to plate 17 for color details. The finished size of the case is 4¼ inches by 6¼ inches.

Materials
#12 mono or interlock canvas, 2 pieces, 7½ inches by
    9½ inches each
Lining fabric, 5½ inches by 13½ inches
1 matching button

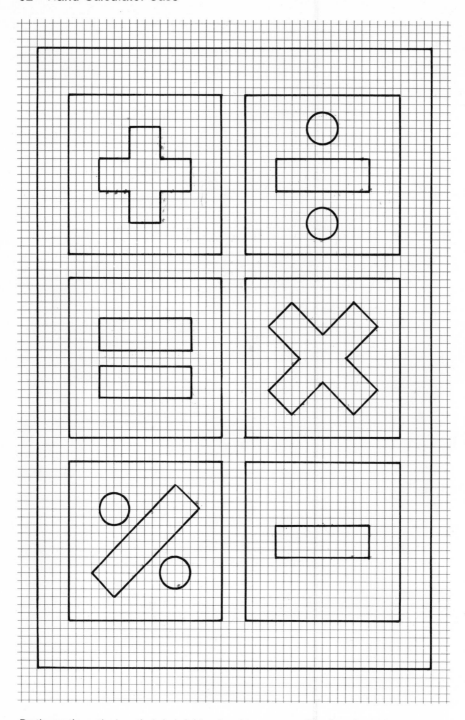

Do the mathematical symbols in bright red on blue squares. The lines between the squares are black and so is the border.

Yarn 33-inch lengths
- 8 red
- 24 blue
- 24 black

Directions

1. Transfer the design to canvas, centering it to leave even sides. The same design is repeated on the front and the back. Stain or paint the design.
2. Stitch the symbols first, then the black lines and border, and then the blue squares. Block the needlepoint.
3. Trim the canvas to ½ of an inch from yarn edge. If mono canvas was used, machine-stitch the canvas edge.
4. Turn the canvas edge under, leaving one row of canvas exposed on the sides and bottom. Turn the top edge and three rows of stitching to the back. Baste.
5. Whipstitch the sides and bottoms of the front and back pieces together.
6. Fold the lining fabric in half, right sides facing, to form a 5½-inch by 6¾-inch rectangle. Machine-stitch the sides together, leaving a ½-inch seam allowance.
7. Without turning the lining right side out, slip it into the case. Turn the top edge of the lining under and blindstitch it to the yarn.
8. If you wish to be able to close up the case, a button can be added to the center top of front panel and a yarn loop added to the center top of back panel. See page 23.

Black and White Purse

A simple, go-everywhere purse is this one-piece purse with narrow-boxed sides. The design is also very effective when done in navy and white or in very dark brown and white. A zipper closes the top. Either use the purse as a clutch bag or attach a loop, shoulder strap, or over-the-arm handle; these can be made of fabric, leather, chain, or ribbon. The handle used here is an 18-inch chain with small rings on each end. Sew end rings to each side of the purse, ½ of an inch down from the top edge. The finished size of the purse is 5 inches by 8 inches.

Materials

#12 mono or interlock canvas,
    12 inches by 14 inches
Lining fabric, 10 inches by 12 inches
9-inch zipper
Handle

The dimensions of the design. Center the design on the canvas and mark the notches, which are not to be stitched, from the full-scale design.

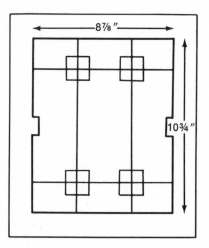

Design for the black and white purse. When you transfer this to canvas, trace one side and then turn the design over to trace the other side, being careful to line up the notches.

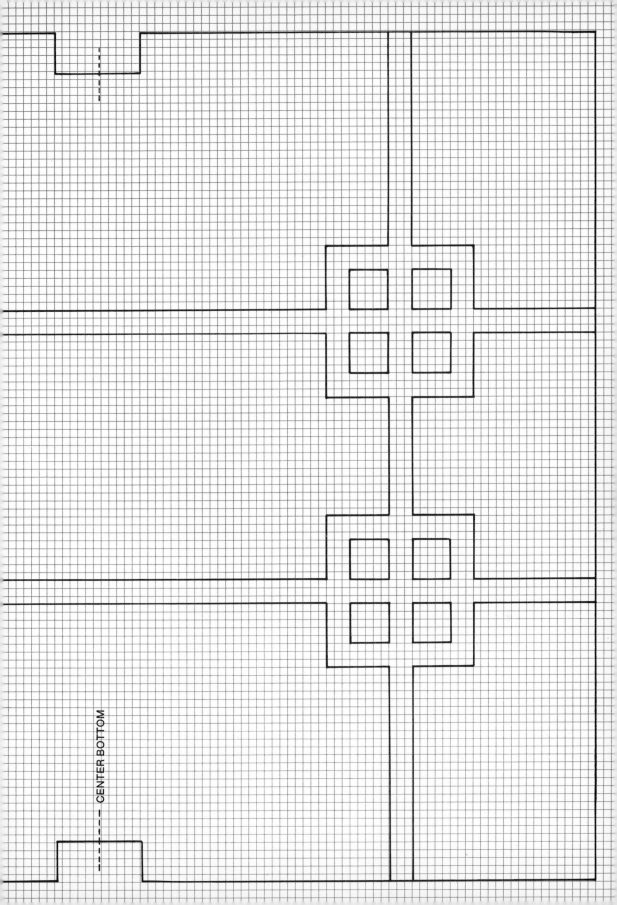

CENTER BOTTOM

Yarn 33-inch lengths
20 white
80 black

Directions

1. Draw the outline of the design, as shown in the drawing on page 94; transfer the design to canvas. Stain or paint the design.
2. Stitch the white areas first and then stitch the black background. Block the needlepoint.
3. Trim the canvas to ½ of an inch from the yarn edge; do not cut the unworked notches at the sides.
4. Fold the canvas edges on the sides under and baste, leaving one row of canvas exposed for joining. Do not baste across the unstitched notched section.
5. Fold the sides to meet, fold canvas at unstitched notched sections to the inside, and whipstitch across bottom, as shown in the drawing. Whipstitch the sides together, changing from black to white as necessary.
6. Turn canvas edge and one row of stitching across the top opening to the inside, and then baste.
7. To install zipper:
   a. Fold side ends at the top to match boxed look of the bottom.
   b. Starting at the opening end of the zipper, hand sew the binding of zipper across its end to the boxed side of the purse.
   c. Continue to hand sew the zipper to yarn edge around the top opening, stitching as close to the binding edge as possible to keep the boxed look. Allow any extra length of zipper to fall inside the purse.
8. Fold lining in half, right sides together, and machine-stitch, leaving a ½-inch seam allowance. To box the corners, place side seams one on top of the other, as shown in the drawing and stitch across. Repeat for second corner.
9. Turn purse inside out. With wrong sides facing, slip the lining over purse. Turn top edges of the lining under and blindstitch to the purse at zipper edge. Turn right side out.

Sewing the unstitched canvas to form the box at the bottom of bag

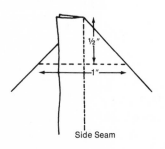

Boxing the lining

Sewing Kit

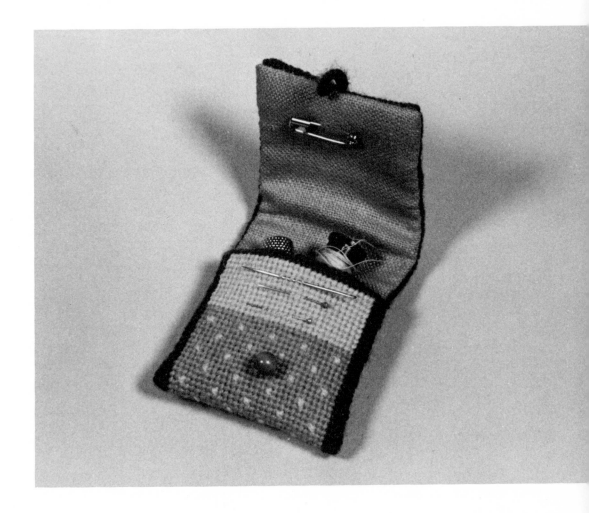

This easy-to-make yellow, orange, and brown sewing kit holds a pair of scissors, thread, thimble, pins, and needles and can be easily slipped into a travel case or purse. Turn to plate 15 for color details. The finished size is 2½ inches by 3¼ inches.

Materials
#12 mono or interlock canvas, 6 inches by 11½ inches
Lining fabric, 3¾ inches by 9½ inches
1 button

The cross-stitches are yellow as is the horizontal panel at the bottom, which will form the top inside portion of the kit when it is folded up. The border is brown and the background is orange.

Yarn   33-inch lengths
    4   yellow
    6   brown
  16   orange

Directions

1. Transfer the design to canvas, centering it. Stain or paint the design.
2. Stitch the yellow cross-stitches first (see page 17) and then the brown border; fill in the yellow panel at the bottom of the design and then the orange background. Block the needlepoint.
3. Trim canvas to ½ of an inch from the yarn edge. If mono canvas was used, machine-stitch the canvas edge.
4. Turn the edges of lining under and place on the back side of canvas.
5. Blindstitch lining to the canvas, covering canvas almost completely, but leaving one row of canvas exposed on the kit sides for joining.
6. Fold the bottom edge up 2¼ inches to form the kit. Whipstitch the sides of this section together.
7. Attach a double strand of yarn to the center of the flap end and buttonhole stitch over the yarn loop, as shown on page 23. Sew a button onto the center bottom of sewing kit.

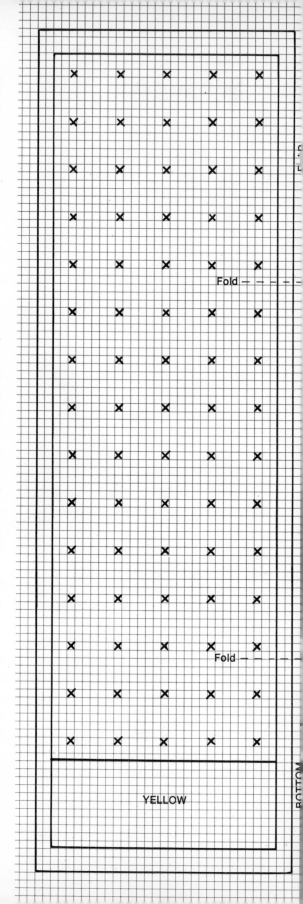

Hearts Set—Purse, Manicure Case, and Contact-Lens Case

The hearts in this design are red, red orange, and magenta. They are placed so that the three different shades of hearts form a diagonal pattern across the white panels. The border and vertical lines are done in a blue purple. Turn to plate 16 to see color details.

This design can be adjusted to fit a square or rectangle of different sizes just by adding or subtracting rows of hearts. Be sure, though, that there are always eleven stitches across the vertical white panels and two rows of stitches across the vertical purple lines. The purple border is three stitches wide.

Purse

This small purse provides a fine way to keep track of grocery coupons, lists, a small engagement book, cosmetics, or just about

Design for one side of the purse. Transfer the design twice, centering it on each piece of canvas. When you paint or stain the hearts, continue in the red, magenta, and red orange sequence as you go down the panels.

anything you wish to keep together in a handbag. The finished size is 4½ inches by 5¾ inches.

Materials

#12 mono or interlock canvas, 2 pieces, 7 inches by
    8½ inches each
2 pieces of lining fabric, the same size as needlepoint
    plus ½ of an inch all around for seam
7-inch nylon zipper

Yarn   33-inch lengths

  6   red   R

  6   red orange   ROR

  6   magenta   M

18   purple

20   white

Directions

1. Transfer the outline, border, vertical lines, and heart shapes to the two pieces of canvas. Paint or stain the design.
2. Stitch the purple border (three stitches wide) and the vertical purple bars (two stitches wide) first. Be sure that there are eleven rows of canvas between the purple vertical bars; then stitch the hearts, following the graph. Fill in the white background and block.
3. Trim the canvas to ½ of an inch from the yarn edge. If mono canvas was used, machine-stitch canvas edge.
4. Turn the canvas and one row of stitching to the back on the top edge of both pieces and baste.
5. With right sides facing up, baste the top edges of both pieces to either side of the zipper. Let the excess length of zipper extend beyond one end of the purse top.
6. With sewing thread, whipstitch across the end of the zipper ½ of an inch from the purse side. Cut the zipper off ¾ of an inch from the whipstitching.
7. Machine-stitch or hand sew zipper in place by sewing one row inside yarn stitching. Fold canvas edges on sides and bottom to the back and baste.
8. Turn needlepoint face down (still flat) and sew in lining by blindstitching to canvas. Leave one line of canvas exposed for joining.
9. Fold purse together with linings facing inside and whipstitch sides and bottom together.

Manicure Case

The size of this easy-to-make roll-up manicure case can be changed by adding or subtracting a row or two of hearts. Sew the lining compartments according to what you need for your own special set of tools. The finished size is 6½ inches by 5 inches.

Materials

#12 mono or interlock canvas, 8½ inches by 10 inches
Lining fabric, 7½ inches by 14 inches
Velvet ribbon, 18 inches long and ¼ of an inch wide

Yarn   33-inch lengths

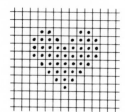

     5   red R
     5   red orange   ROR
     5   magenta M
   15   purple
   16   white

Directions

1. Transfer the outline, lines, and hearts to the canvas.
2. Stitch the purple border (three stitches wide) and the vertical bars (two stitches wide) first. Be sure that there are eleven rows of canvas between the purple lines. Stitch the hearts following the graph. Fill in the white background and block.
3. Trim the canvas to ½ of an inch from the yarn edge. If mono canvas was used, machine-stitch canvas edge.
4. Turn canvas and three rows of the border to the back on all sides, and baste.
5. To make the lining:

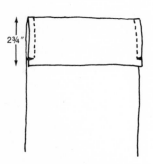

Folding and sewing
top edge of lining

a. Fold the top 2¾ inches down over the front. Sew the sides of this section, from the fold to ½ of an inch from the edge, as shown in the drawing.
b. Clip the seam at end of stitched line. Turn the flap and press.
c. Sew across the flap at clipped edges, as shown in the drawing.

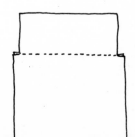

Sewing the turned and
clipped flap

The design for the manicure case. Transfer it, centering it on the piece of canvas.
When you paint or stain the hearts continue the red, magenta, and red orange sequence
as you go down the panels.

Sewing across folded
bottom edge

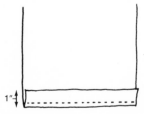

d. Fold the bottom edge up 1 inch; stitch across bottom, ¼ of an inch from the fold, as shown in the drawing.

e. Place the lining on canvas, with the wrong sides together and the stitching of the top fold lined up with the top of the canvas.

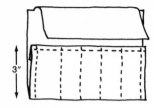

Pinning and basting
the pockets in the lining

3″

f. Fold the bottom lining up, 3 inches, and adjust to fit the canvas. Remove the fabric and pin the sides together. Pin and baste the pockets to fit the tools, as shown in the drawing. Machine-stitch the compartments and sides.

g. Turn the side edges under, ½ of an inch, and baste.

6. Fold the ribbon, 6 inches from one end, and pin it to the wrong side of the canvas at the center of one side, as shown in the drawing.

7. Place the lining on the canvas back and baste all around all edges, catching the ribbon between the lining and canvas.

8. Blindstitch the lining to yarn edge.

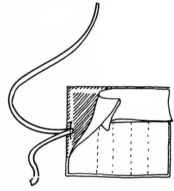

Placing the ribbon and basting the lining to the finished needlepoint

Contact-Lens Case

A small purselike case can have many uses. This particular one is designed as a contact-lens case, but could hold coins, bus tokens, or stamps. The finished size is 3 inches by 3½ inches.

Materials
#12 mono or interlock canvas, 6½ inches by 11 inches
Lining fabric, 4½ inches by 8¾ inches
1 button

Yarn   33-inch lengths
    4   red   R
    4   red orange   ROR
    4   magenta   M
  12   purple
  12   white

The design for the contact-lens case. Transfer it, centering it on the piece of canvas.
When you paint or stain the hearts continue the red orange, red, and magenta
sequence down the panels.

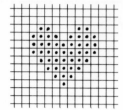

Directions

1. Transfer the outline, border, vertical lines, and heart design to the canvas. Paint or stain the design.
2. Stitch the purple border (three stitches wide) and vertical bars (two stitches wide) first. Be sure there are eleven rows of canvas between the purple lines for the heart pattern. Stitch the hearts, following the graph. Fill in the white background and block.
3. Trim canvas to ½ of an inch from the yarn edge. If mono canvas was used, machine-stitch canvas edge.
4. Turn the canvas and one row of stitching to the back on each of the ends and flap sides. Turn the canvas on the sides under, leaving one row of canvas exposed for joining. Baste.
5. Place the lining on the wrong side of canvas. Turn edges under and blindstitch in place. Hide the canvas on flap end and leave one row of canvas exposed on the sides for joining.
6. Fold the bottom up 2¾ inches and whipstitch the sides.
7. Attach a double strand of yarn on the center of the flap end. Buttonhole stitch over the yarn loop, as shown in the drawing on page 23.
8. Sew on the button.

Wedding
Photo Album

Words stitched in needlepoint make a project personal and special. This is a patch (Method A) or inset (Method B) for a wedding album, but could be used on a wedding pillow or framed wall panel, as well. The colors and design chosen for a wedding design are important. Tom and Ritva had an outdoor, spring wedding in the foothills. Ritva wore a dress from her native Finland. The blue and green in the design represent the season and the location, while the folk designs echo the embroidery in Ritva's dress. Turn to plate 10 for color details, and to pages 13 and 14 for graphs of the two alphabets used here. The finished size of the needlepoint is 5 inches by 7 inches.

Materials
#12 mono or interlock canvas, 8 inches by 10 inches
Graph paper
Photo album
Cover fabric, ½ of a yard synthetic suede (Method B only)
Felt fabric to fit inside album cover (Method B only)

Yarn   33-inch lengths (Adjust if you are using other designs)
- 2   light blue
- 2   cream
- 3   pink
- 2   dark pink
- 26   green

Directions

1. Draw a 5-inch by 7-inch outline on the center of your canvas. Use graph paper to plan the lettering and design placement. See pages 13 and 14 for alphabets. Depending upon how much room the lettering takes up, the flowers and hearts can be used for the border design. Transfer the design you are using to canvas; paint or stain the design or use the graph for a guide. In this needlepoint panel the hearts are pink, the flower petals are dark pink, and the stems and leaves are pink. The lettering is in cream and light blue, while the background is green.
2. Stitch the design and block.
3. Choose one of the following methods for finishing.

Method A—Patch

1. Carefully cut canvas one row away from the stitching on edges.
2. Overcast stitch the edges on all sides.
3. Spread a light layer of fabric glue on the back of the patch and attach it to the center front of the photo album.

Method B—Inset

1. Trim the canvas to 1 inch from the yarn edge. If mono canvas was used, machine-stitch the canvas edge.
2. With the book closed, measure the height and distance around the album (across front, past binding edge, and across back). Add 3 inches to each total for the cover fabric measurement; cut this fabric. The album used here is 11½ inches high and 9½ inches across with a 1-inch binding, so the cover fabric was cut 14½ inches by 23 inches.
3. Place the album in the center of the wrong side of fabric. Wrap fabric around album and fold the edges inside the cover. Hold fabric edges to inside of the cover with masking tape.
4. Center the needlepoint on the album front; mark the four

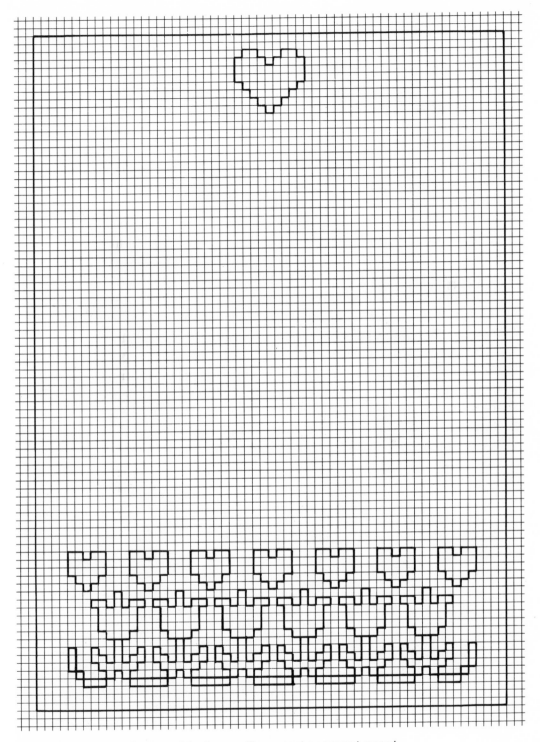

Graph for stitching the hearts and the flowers. These may be arranged around
the lettering any way you wish.

corners of the needlepoint design on the fabric with straight pins. Remove the needlepoint and check the pin placement. They should mark the corners of a 5-inch by 7-inch rectangle. With a pencil, lightly draw the rectangle on the cover fabric, making sure that that the lines are parallel to the album edge.

5. Remove fabric from the album and carefully cut out the rectangle. If the fabric is synthetic suede, there is no need to turn the edges of the opening under.

6. Center the needlepoint on album front and attach it with fabric glue.

7. Lightly spread the fabric glue on the canvas edge next to yarn stitching. Place the opening of the cover fabric over the needlepoint; press edges to bond with the glued canvas edge. Allow to dry.

8. Apply a light layer of glue to the binding. Close the album and gently fold the cover fabric over the binding edge to the back.

9. Fold the edges of fabric to the inside of cover and glue. Clip fabric at the binding edge so that cover fabric can be glued and tucked into the binding section.

10. Cut two pieces of lightweight felt to fit inside the covers. Each should be 1 inch less than the height and ½ of an inch less than the width.

11. Spread a light layer of fabric glue on felt and attach it to the inside of the covers. The felt will extend to ½ of an inch from outside edges.

Floral Purse

A metal purse handle, this one 5 inches wide, holds a floral print of bright oranges, gold, yellow, pink, and olive. The purse is made in one piece and the seams are machine-stitched. Turn to plate 13 for color details. The finished size of the purse is 6 inches by 7 inches.

Materials
#12 mono or interlock canvas, 9½ inches by 17 inches
5-inch curved handle frame
Lining, the same size as needlepoint, plus ½ of an inch all
    around for seam

Yarn   33-inch lengths

3	yellow Y	15	olive OL
4	yellow orange YOR	14	pink P
15	orange OR	20	gold GD
12	red orange ROR		

Design for floral purse

Directions

1. Transfer the design to canvas, centering it. Stain or paint the design.
2. Stitch the design, starting with the smaller elements. Block the needlepoint.

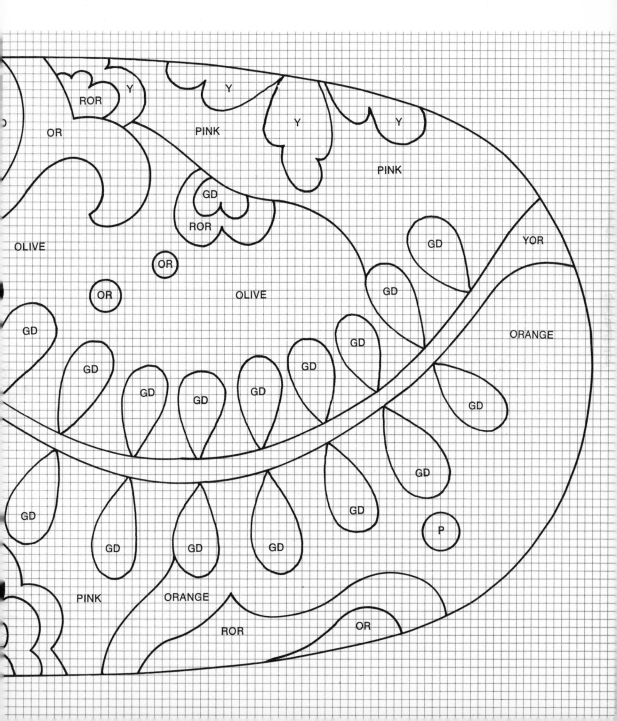

3. Trim the canvas to ½ of an inch from the yarn edge. If you have used mono canvas, machine-stitch canvas edge.

4. Fold the needlepoint in half, right sides facing. Baste the side seams together, two rows inside the yarn edge. End the seam where the handle will be attached. Machine-stitch the sides.

5. Turn right side out. Fold the top curves edge under and baste.

6. Sew needlepoint to outside of the handle frame.

7. Fold the lining in half, right sides facing, and stitch the side seams.

8. Without turning, slip lining into purse. Turn top edges under and stitch to handle, using the same holes used to attach the purse.

Camera Case and Strap

This rainbow design is a simple rectangle of needlepoint combined with vinyl sides to make a case for an Instamatic camera. The zipper and strap holders are sewn to the vinyl before the needlepoint panel is added. Turn to plate 18 for color details. The finished size of this case is 5½ inches by 3¼ inches with 2½-inch sides; the size can be changed, however, for other cameras.

Camera Case

Materials

#12 mono or interlock canvas, 8½ inches by 11½ inches
Vinyl; 1 piece, 3¾ inches by 12½ inches for top and sides;
     2 pieces, ¾ of an inch by 4½ inches, for strap holders
9-inch zipper
Lining fabric, 6¾ inches by 9¾ inches
2 half-circle rings, 1 inch wide

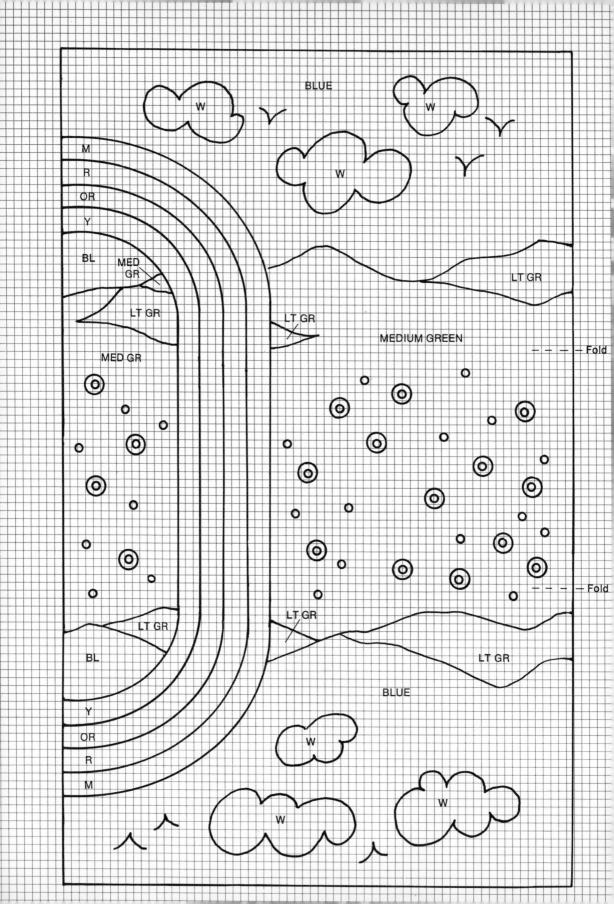

Design for the camera case. Almost all the elements
are color-labeled. The birds are dark blue. The
flowers are white with yellow centers, and the
small dots are random yellow and white.

Yarn   33-inch lengths

1	dark blue		3	light green LT GR
2	yellow Y		14	medium green MED GR
2	orange OR		4	white W
2	red R		18	blue BL
3	magenta M			

Directions
1. Transfer the design to canvas and stain or paint.
2. Stitch the design, starting with the smaller elements, and block.
3. Trim the canvas to ¾ of an inch from the yarn edge. If mono canvas was used, machine-stitch canvas edge.
4. See the drawing for the placement of strap holders and zipper on the vinyl. Cut the zipper opening 9 inches long and ¼ of an inch wide. Put the zipper under the opening, and, without turning the edges under, stitch it in place.
5. Slip half-circle rings on one end of each vinyl strap piece. Do not turn the sides of strap pieces under. Fold the ends of strap pieces over 1 inch, and glue to the back of the strap piece with fabric glue. Place on the vinyl, as shown in the drawing, and topstitch by machine.
6. With right sides facing, baste the needlepoint to the vinyl piece, leaving zipper open for turning. Match corners of the vinyl with the fold lines on the needlepoint design. Clip at corners when necessary.

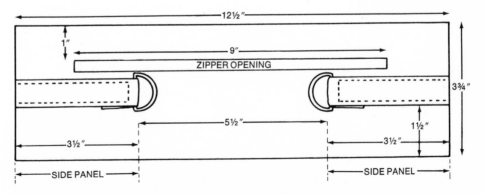

Pattern for the top and sides of the camera case
showing the placement of the zipper and the strap holders

7. With canvas side up machine-stitch along the outside row of yarn stitching.
8. Fold edges of the lining fabric under, and blindstitch to the wrong side of the needlepoint. Do not line vinyl sides.
9. Turn right side out.

Camera-Case Strap

This rainbow camera-case strap wraps over the shoulder, echoing the colors of the camera case. Vinyl fabric and swivel hooks complete the strap. The finished size is 1½ inches by 32½ inches, plus vinyl and hooks.

Materials

#12 mono or interlock canvas, 5 inches by 36 inches
Vinyl fabric, 4 inches by 6 inches
2 swivel hooks
Grosgrain ribbon, 1½ inches by 34 inches

Yarn   33-inch lengths

   12   yellow
   10   orange
   10   red
   28   blue

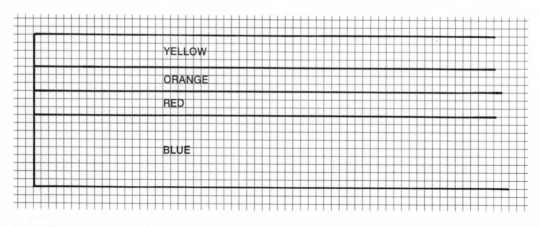

YELLOW

ORANGE

RED

BLUE

Design for the camera-case strap. Continue the lines for the stripes for 32½ inches.

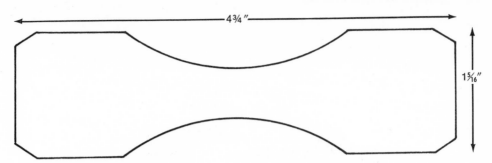

Full-size pattern for vinyl strap ends

Directions

1. Transfer the design to the canvas. Continue the stripes for the 32½ inches; stain or paint the design.
2. Stitch the design and block.
3. Trim canvas to ½ of an inch from the yarn edge. If mono canvas was used, machine-stitch canvas edge. Turn canvas edges on sides and ends to back and baste.
4. Cut vinyl strap ends, following the pattern. Fold strap ends in half and slip one hook onto each strap end. Machine-stitch across the folded end next to the hook as shown in drawing.
5. Place a vinyl strap end under each end of the needlepoint strap. Overlay ¾ of an inch onto the canvas and then baste.
6. Face back of canvas with grosgrain ribbon, turning the ends of ribbon under; the edges of the ribbon are finished so don't turn under. Blindstitch ribbon to sides.
7. Secure vinyl strap ends to the needlepoint strap by hand sewing or machine-stitching across the ends through all layers.

Folding the strap ends
through swivel hook,
and machine-stitching
to secure them

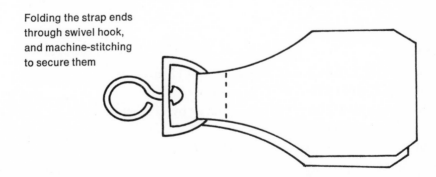

Jewelry Case

This case, with its zippered pockets for pieces of jewelry and a fabric bar for rings, is a wonderful aid to the traveler. It is small and compact, so it can be easily carried in a purse or suitcase. Turn to plate 1 for the color details. The finished size is 6 inches by 8½ inches.

Materials

#12 mono or interlock canvas, 9 inches by 11½ inches
2 zippers, each 4 inches long (See step 4b)
3 pieces of lining fabric; 2 pieces, 7 inches by 9½ inches,
    1 piece, 1 inch by 5½ inches
Velvet ribbon, 20 inches
Velcro dot

The jewelry case desig

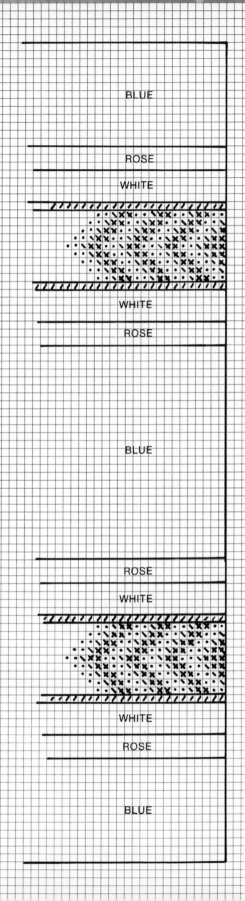

Yarn 33-inch lengths

   2 dark rose /

   3 dark green ✕

 12 white ＼

 12 rose •

 22 blue

Directions

1. Transfer the outline and main lines of the design to canvas. Stain or paint the background areas. See the drawing for dimensions and the arrangement of stripes.
2. Following the graph, stitch the design. Block the needlepoint.
3. Trim the canvas to ½ of an inch from yarn edge. If mono canvas was used, machine-stitch the canvas edge. Turn canvas and one row of stitching on all sides to the back; baste.

Continue stitching the design across the 6-inch width of the case.

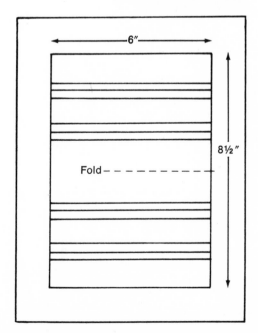

4. To make the lining:

a. Use a nonraveling fabric, such as imitation suede, for the top lining so that you will not have to turn under the zipper openings. A lighter weight fabric can be used for the inside lining.

b. Make a 4-inch-long slit for the zippers, 1¼ inches from each end of the lining, as shown in the drawing. Trim cut so that it is ⅛ of an inch wide. (If you cannot find 4-inch zippers, cut a 7-inch nylon zipper to 4½ inches long and whipstitch the ends with sewing thread to hold in place.) Baste and then machine-stitch the zippers in lining.

Inserting the zippers in the lining

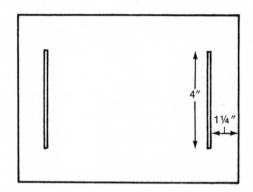

c. Place the top and bottom linings, right sides together, and baste all edges. Machine-stitch with a ½-inch seam allowance around the edges, leaving a 3-inch opening on one side for turning. Remove bastings.

d. Turn the lining right side out. Turn the edges of the 3-inch opening to the inside. Baste the edges and then topstitch by hand or machine, ⅛ of an inch from the edge on all sides.

e. Machine-stitch across the lining at the center to create two pockets, as shown in the drawing.

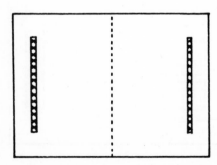

Stitching across
the double lining to form
two pockets

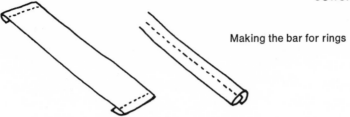

Making the bar for rings

f. Cut a strip of lining cloth, 1 inch by 5½ inches, for the ring strap; turn each end under, ¼ of an inch, and topstitch. Fold one long side under, ⅝ of an inch, and press. Fold the other long side over the first and then baste, as shown in the drawing. Machine-stitch down the center of the strap.

g. Attach one end of the strap to the side of lining at center seam. Sew a Velcro dot to the other end of the strap. Find the proper position for the other part of the dot and sew it in place on the lining.

5. Place lining on back of the canvas. Attach ribbon at the center of each side, ½ of an inch into seam, between lining and canvas. Baste all edges. Blindstitch the lining and ribbon to canvas.

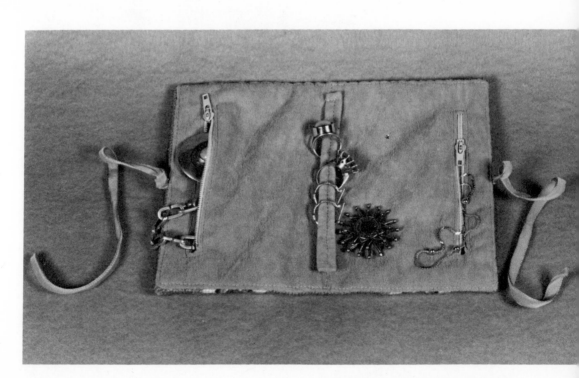

The inside of the finished jewelry case

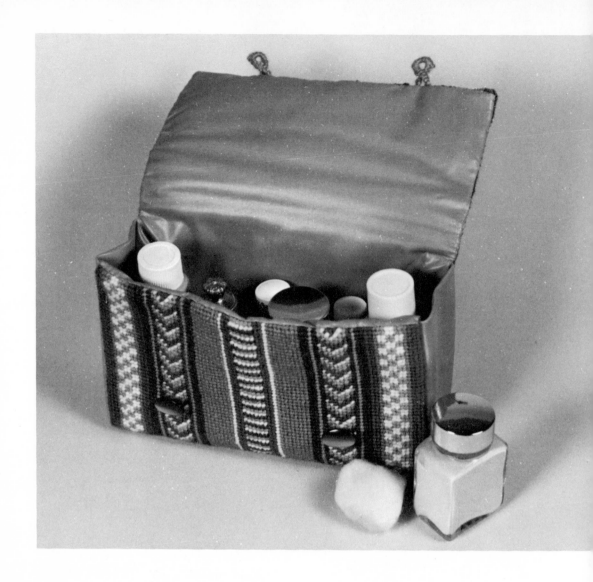

Travel Makeup Case

An inset of vinyl fabric forms the sides and bottom of this makeup case, giving it a boxed shape that is convenient for carrying small jars and bottles. The fold-over flap holds everything in place and the waterproof lining is easy to wipe clean. This design, without the vinyl inset, can be sewn together for an attractive clutch bag. Turn to plate 14 for the color detail. The finished size is 4 inches by 7 inches with 2-inch sides.

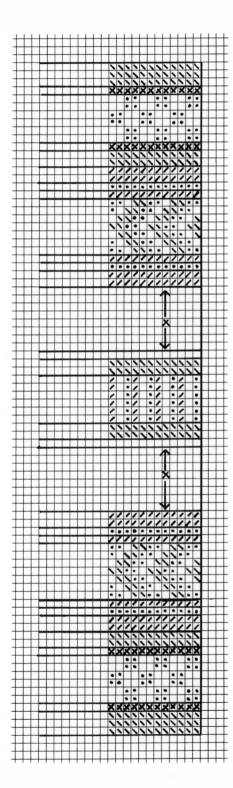

Materials

#12 mono or interlock canvas;
   1 piece 7 inches by 10 inches, and
   1 piece, 10 inches by 11 inches
Vinyl inset fabric, 3 inches by 17
   inches
2 buttons
Waterproof lining fabric; 2 pieces
   the same size as needlepoint
   pattern plus ½ of an inch all
   around for seam; 1 piece, 3
   inches by 17 inches, for inset

Yarn   33-inch lengths
   21   green \
   18   pink •
   15   wine /
   15   white
   22   lavender ✕

Directions

1. Transfer the outline and vertical
   lines of the design to canvas and
   stain or paint the areas within the
   lines.
2. Stitch the design on the front and
   back panels, following the graph for
   design details. There is no code for
   areas to be stitched in white. Block
   the needlepoint.

The makeup case design.
Continue stitching the design
to cover both panels.

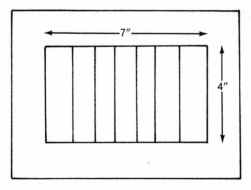

Front panel

Back and flap panel

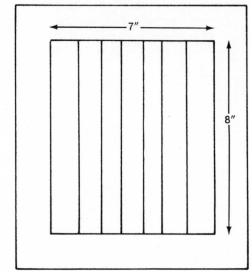

3. Trim canvas to ½ of an inch from the yarn edge. If mono canvas was used, machine-stitch the canvas edge.

4. Baste the front panel to side inset, right sides together. Clip the corners if necessary. The vinyl sides will extend 1 inch above the yarn edge on each side of the front panel. Using a long stitch, machine-sew in the outside row of yarn stitching.

5. With right sides facing, baste the back panel to the vinyl inset in the same manner as you did the front, lining up the bottom corners of the back panel with the bottom corners of the front panel. Leave the top 1 inch of vinyl sides unstitched. Clip the corners, if necessary, and machine-sew with a long stitch in the outside row of yarn stitching. Turn right side out.

6. Turn the edges of canvas and one row of stitching to the inside on the flap and baste. Turn the top edge of canvas on the front panel to the inside and baste. Turn the side vinyl ends to the inside and glue with fabric glue. The sides and the front should be the same height.

7. Sew the lining together in the same way that you did the outside. Without turning, slip lining inside the case. Turn edges of the lining under; blindstitch to the canvas and side fabric.

The travel makeup case when it is closed

8. Fold the flap over the front. Position and sew on buttons, one on each side of center, to the front panel. For button loops, attach a double strand of yarn on the flap. Buttonhole stitch over the yarn loops as shown on page 23.